GOING TO SCHOOL IN THE MIDDLE EAST AND NORTH AFRICA

GOING TO SCHOOL IN THE MIDDLE EAST AND NORTH AFRICA

KWABENA DEI OFORI-ATTAH

The Global School Room
Alan Sadovnik and Susan Semel, Series Editors

GREENWOOD PRESS
Westport, Connecticut • London

Library of Congress Cataloging-in-Publication Data

Ofori-Attah, Kwabena Dei, 1949–
    Going to school in the Middle East and North Africa / Kwabena Dei Ofori-Attah.
        p. cm. — (The global school room, ISSN 1933–6101)
    Includes bibliographical references and index.
    ISBN-13: 978–0–313–34294–3 (alk. paper)
    1. Education—Middle East. 2. Education—Africa, North. I. Title.
    LA1430.2.O36 2008
    370.956—dc22   2008016570

British Library Cataloguing in Publication Data is available.

Library of Congress Catalog Card Number: 2008016570
ISBN-13: 978–0–313–34294–3
ISSN: 1933–6101

First published in 2008

Greenwood Press, 88 Post Road West, Westport, CT 06881
An imprint of Greenwood Publishing Group, Inc.
www.greenwood.com

Printed in the United States of America

BOOK
×65.00

The paper used in this book complies with the
Permanent Paper Standard issued by the National
Information Standards Organization (Z39.48–1984).

10 9 8 7 6 5 4 3 2 1

193175605

CONTENTS

SERIES FOREWORD

Over the past three decades, with globalization becoming a dominant force, the worldwide emphasis on schooling has accelerated. However, a historical perspective teaches us that global trends in schooling are by no means a recent phenomenon. The work of neoinstitutional sociologists such as John Meyer and his colleagues has demonstrated that the development of mass public educational systems became a worldwide trend in the nineteenth century and most nations' schools systems go back significantly further. The Going to School around the World series is intended to provide students with an understanding of the similarities and differences among educational systems throughout the world from a historical perspective.

Although comparative and international educational research has provided an understanding of the many similarities in school systems across nations and cultures, it has also indicated the significant differences. Schools reflect societies and their cultures and therefore there are significant differences among different nations' school systems and educational practices. Another purpose of this series is to examine these similarities and differences.

The series is organized into nine volumes, each looking at the history of the school systems in countries on one continent or subcontinent. The series consists of volumes covering schooling in the following regions:

North America
Latin America
Europe
Sub-Saharan Africa
North Africa and the Middle East
South Asia

Central Asia
East Asia
Oceania

As the sixth volume in the series to be published, *Going to School in the Middle East and North Africa* by Kwabena Dei Ofori-Attah provides an important and timely examination of important comparisons of the educational systems in the Middle East and North Africa. Organized thematically, rather than by country as in the previous volumes, this book examines the similarities and differences among different systems with respect to school organization, the history of their educational systems, the relationship between religion and schooling, issues of education and inequality, the relationship between education and development, and the education of various groups, including ethnic and religious minorities, women, and the handicapped. Through the history of the educational systems in different countries and an analysis of contemporary systems, the author provides a rich description of how schooling is related to national culture, religion, identity, and social, political, and economic structures and economic development. Moreover, the book illustrates the importance of historical, philosophical, and sociological perspectives in understanding the similarities and differences among societies and their schools. Finally, the book provides everyday examples of what schools in each country are like and how curriculum and teaching practices reflect the larger cultural, social, religious, and historical patterns of each society.

Going to School in the Middle East and North Africa is emblematic of the series in that it provides students with an understanding that schooling needs to be understood in the context of each local culture, rather than viewed ethnocentrically from a United States or Western perspective. We often tend to make broad generalizations about other continents and assume that culture and schooling are uniform across countries. This book demonstrates the importance of examining national systems to uncover differences, as well as similarities.

In *The Japanese Educational Challenge* (1987), Merry White argued that the purpose of studying another country's educational system is not necessarily to copy it, but rather to learn from the lessons of other societies, and where appropriate to use these lessons to improve our own schools. *Going to School in the Middle East and North Africa* provides many important lessons, but it also cautions us to understand these in the context of national and cultural differences.

Finally, in an area of the world where historical and ongoing religious and ethnic conflict and violence continue to define daily existence, the role of education in exacerbating or reducing such conflict is a crucial issue. In a recent lecture at the City College of New York, Nobel Laureate Elie Wiesel stated that respect for all religions is vital to ending ethnic and religious conflict and genocidal violence around the world—and that education must play a key role in socializing children to love and respect others different than themselves rather than hate them due to historical memories. Although he acknowledged the difficulty in accomplishing this, it is evident that an understanding of the role of schooling in each country included in this book provides an important beginning.

We invite you to continue to explore schooling around the world, this time in the Middle East and North Africa.

Alan Sadovnik and Susan Semel

REFERENCE

White, M. (1987). *The Japanese Educational Challenge*. New York: The Free Press.

PREFACE

The Middle East and North Africa region, often called the "MENA countries" for short, stretches from the Atlantic coast to beyond the ancient Euphrates River. This part of the world is often referred to as the cradle of our modern civilization.

This book, *Going to School in the Middle East and North Africa*, is one of a series on the global schoolroom. The contents of this book cover educational progress in several countries in the region, including Algeria, Bahrain, Egypt, Israel, Lebanon, Libya, Morocco, Qatar, Saudi Arabia, Syria, Tunisia, Turkey, the United Arab Emirates, and Yemen. These nations are held together by religion, culture, and language. It is therefore no wonder that many of the countries in the region cooperate in making modern schooling facilities available to all the children in the region.

The Middle East and North Africa accounts for more than 50 percent of the world's crude oil supply, and it is also known to possess about 65 percent of oil reserves. Saudi Arabia, the leading oil producer in the world, is located in this region. Most of the MENA countries often use part of their oil revenues to improve educational infrastructure. Bahrain, Saudi Arabia, Kuwait, and the United Arab Emirates, for example, have made significant progress in their infrastructure and consequently in education. These developments have often affected reforms in education.

Today, nearly all the industrialized nations have set up schools in the region to help shape its teaching and learning. Great Britain, France, Germany, Japan, and the United States have all established schools there to offer Western-style education to millions of children, most of them foreigners living in the region. These foreign educational institutions cover the kindergarten through university levels. The curriculum each foreign school uses must follow guidelines set up by the host government. This is done to preserve local interests and culture in the educational system.

Education at all levels has undergone tremendous reforms in recent years. These reforms followed government legislations that were implemented around the early 1970s.

One area in which the region has made significant progress is gender education. All the MENA countries have introduced legislation that promotes equality of educational opportunities for both male and female students. There has, therefore, been significant female enrollment in nearly all the countries in the entire region. Special needs education has also gained the attention of the area's governments. Children who need special attention no longer have to rely solely on their family resources to receive education. All the governments throughout the region have recognized the right of all children to receive appropriate education. In many cases, education is free up to the high school level, and in some cases, up to the university level.

In the area of educational technology, the Middle East and North Africa can boast of the best in every category of modern technological tools for teaching and learning. Children going to school in the region have access to computers and the Internet, digital cameras, email, scanners, and course management systems such as Blackboard.

The region is vast and complex. What may be true in one region may not be the case in others. In this book, examples of innovative curriculum practices have been selected from as many countries as possible to give an accurate picture of what children are learning in most of the schools in the Middle East and North Africa.

ACKNOWLEDGMENTS

This book is the result of the collective efforts of several people and agencies. Without their help, you might not be reading this book. Some of them may not even be aware that the information they shared and discussed with me about the Middle East and North Africa (MENA) about ten years ago still remains in me like an oasis, never drying up, and springing forth in me as fresh ideas about the region.

One area that intrigues me about the MENA region is the steady progress being made in education. Although the region can boast of being a pioneer in formal schooling, for several decades schooling facilities there fell short of public expectations. However, the discovery of oil has changed the face of education in nearly all the countries that form part of his huge swath of land, the home of great ancient civilizations.

Indeed, I am forever grateful to all of them for helping me gain a greater insight into a region where innovative practices in organized learning, technology, and economic activities in the past have changed educational systems throughout the world today.

I would like to thank Dr. Gifford Doxsee of Ohio University, who first provided me the impetus to undertake this study. As a graduate student at Ohio University, I took several courses with him on the Middle East and North Africa. Each course opened a new avenue for me to understand the history, politics, and social characteristics of the region.

Professor Milton Ploghoft of Ohio University, through my involvement in the activities of the African Educational Research Network, provided me the opportunity to access valuable information for the book.

Of course, I could not have produced this book without the help I received from UNESCO, World Education Services (WES), and the Comparative and International Education Society (CIES). UNESCO provided me with valuable data on current trends in school enrollments in the MENA region. WES gave me current information on educational trends in the region. And CIES placed at my disposal all the information I needed to complete this book.

In gratitude, I would like to thank the numerous North African and Middle Eastern students who participated in this project by answering my questions on the education practices in the region.

On the home front, I would like to thank my wife Elizabeth and my children for bearing with me as I deserted them on numerous occasions to work on the book. I thank my daughter, Maame Serwah Ofori-Attah, for helping me with the organization of the numerous tables.

Chapter 1

NORTH AFRICA AND THE MIDDLE EAST: THE REGION DEFINED

As pointed out by Williams (1968), the "Middle East" as a geographic entity was a term coined by an American historian, A. T. Mahan, in 1902 to denote

a sphere of Western political influence rather than a precise geographical or ethnic area. At its widest extent it is held to include the region from Turkey and the Mediterranean seaboard lands to Jordan, Iraq and Iran in the east, the Arabian peninsula in the south, with Egypt and Sudan on the African continent. (p. 1)

North Africa is bounded by the Sahara Desert in the south and the Mediterranean in the north. Modern North Africa is made up of Algeria, Egypt, Libya, Morocco, and Tunisia, and the Maghrib (western North Africa) comprises Algeria, Libya, Morocco, and Tunisia. Some of the countries in North Africa are also found in the region defined as the Middle East. Countries in the Middle East and North Africa (MENA) include Algeria, Bahrain, Cyprus, Egypt, Iraq, Israel, Jordan, Kuwait, Lebanon, Libya, Morocco, Oman, the Palestinian Authority, Qatar, Saudi Arabia, Sudan, Syria, Tunisia, Turkey, the United Arab Emirates, the Western Sahara, and Yemen. The Middle East is also sometimes referred to as Southwest Asia.

Most of the countries in the MENA region were once part of the Byzantine Empire. Emperor Charlemagne (Charles the Great) is noted for promoting formal schooling in the Byzantine Empire. It is often stated that his interest in education was so great that he looked to the West for a famous educator, Alcuin of York, to manage the schools in the Byzantine Empire. Charlemagne and his family members enrolled in some of the palace schools he established and studied to read and write. During this period, the concept of the seven liberal arts came into use. The seven liberal arts constituted the curriculum that was often used in the schools at the time. They consisted of the *trivium* (grammar, rhetoric, and logic) and the *quadrivium* (arithmetic, geometry, music, and astronomy) (Johnson, Dupuis, Musial, Hall, & Gollnick, 2005). "Liberal arts education" is used today to describe the portion of the curriculum that is not concerned with science, technology, technical, or professional studies (Webb, Metha, & Jordan, 2000).

FOUNDATIONS OF LEARNING IN THE MIDDLE EAST AND NORTH AFRICA

The Middle East and North Africa have a long history of organized learning. It is very hard to determine the exact period when formal schooling started in the region.

Around 3500 B.C., the Sumerians in ancient Mesopotamia used a form of writing called *cuneiform* to communicate. It was named from the Latin word *cuneus,* because of its wedge-shaped characteristics. As the years passed by and the people continued to develop their systems of writing to share ideas, they developed a form of writing that was made up of symbols and sounds. The Sumerians used about six hundred signs to communicate.

Cuneiform numbers were written using a combination of just two signs: a vertical wedge for 1 and a corner wedge for 10. Handwriting varied as much in Old Babylonian times as it does now. The basic system of numbers is illustrated in figure 1.1.

The students wrote on tablets made of clay or papyrus and later on wooden boards or leather. Papyrus was made from plants called *Cyperus papyrus,* just as the paper we use in modern times is made from trees. The students wrote with sharp instruments such as dried reeds. Ink was kept in small pots, and the reeds were dipped in them to absorb it. The ink was made from water, charcoal, or colored mineral (Walker, 2003).

The complex nature of the letters made writing cumbersome and tedious. Teachers sat very close to students to give them the help they needed. The students sat on the floor while learning to write. To the outsider, this posture looked uncomfortable, but once the students got used to it, they felt comfortable in the classroom. Teachers put a lot of emphasis on calligraphy, and so most of the students worked with the skills of an artist (Hartt, 1993).

Ancient Egyptians enrolled people in scribe schools, where they learned how to read and write. Archaeological records indicate that these scribes after graduation worked in the king's palace, in the army as clerks, and in the fields to document agricultural produce. They kept records of all social events, laws, and decisions made by the king concerning legal matters. In all temples, the scribes wrote important messages on the walls to remind people of major past religious or divine events. The Egyptians used special characters called *hieroglyphics* to record their messages (Caldwell & Gyles, 1966). Two cursive versions later came into use. These were the *hieratic* and later *demotic* versions (Hawkins, 1979).

Figure 1.1
Sumerian Numerals

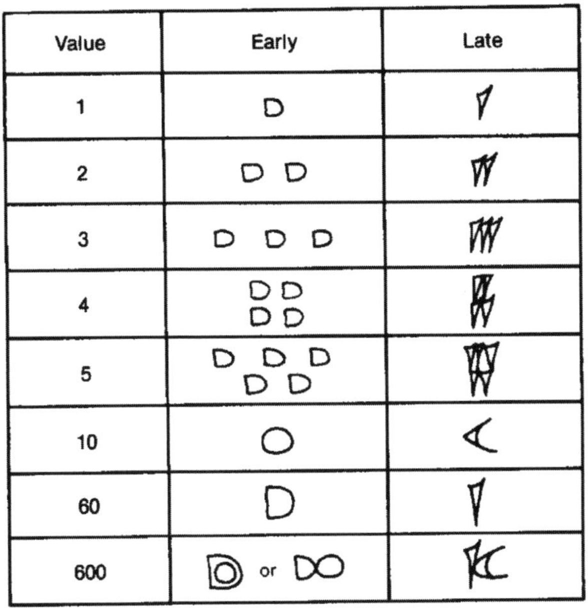

Value	Early	Late
1	D	𝑃
2	D D	𝑊
3	D D D	𝑊
4	D D D D	𝑊
5	D D D D D	𝑊
10	O	<
60	D	𝑉
600	⟟ or D⟨	𝐾

Source: Social Science Staff of the Educational Research Council of America (1982, p. 104).

Hieroglyphic writing was the most sacred of the ancient Egyptian scripts. The term *hieroglyphs* comes from the Greek word for the script. It was only used to record important information about religion or the pharaoh. Hieroglyphs were usually written on the walls of temples and tombs or on stone slabs called *stelae*.

Hieratic script was the common script used in ancient Egypt from about 2600 B.C. to 700 B.C. The word *hieratic* comes from the Greek word (*hieratika*) for the script. Hieratic was used by scribes to write down everyday information, keep records, and write letters.

Another script commonly used in ancient Egypt from about 700 B.C. was demotic. This form of writing was used chiefly for official records, literature, and letters. The word *demotic* comes from the Greek word (*demotika*) for the script.

The Rosetta Stone found in Egypt by the French was designed in 196 B.C. by Egyptian scribes. It was found by a French soldier, Pierre-Francois Bouchard, in 1799 in the port town of Rosetta (now called Rashid) in Egypt. The stone was three feet, nine inches long, two feet, four and half inches wide, and eleven inches thick. It contained three distinct bands of writing, each with different scripts. The inscriptions on the stone were in two languages, Greek and Egyptian. The Egyptian scribes used three scripts to design it: hieroglyphic, demotic, and Greek (Brewer & Teeter, 1999). The scribes used these three scripts because they were the common scripts used at the time. Greek was the language of the rulers.

The Rosetta Stone listed the achievements of the Egyptian pharaoh. It listed all the good things that the Egyptian pharaoh did for his country. It seems that modern resolutions are written in the fashion of the inscriptions on the Rosetta Stone.

The famous Hammurabi Code was designed by scribes in ancient Babylon between 1792 and 1750 B.C. It was designed to provide legal bases for judges in handling cases in the empire. It is generally believed that Hammurabi's code is the basis for the legal system of the world.

The Phoenicians, in present-day Lebanon in the Middle East, are believed to have first used the alphabet as we know it today. They developed the alphabet from the Egyptian hieroglyphics, gave them Semitic names, and added a few of their own scripts (Caldwell & Gyles, 1966). According to Easton (1964), the "oldest known alphabet, dating from about 1400 B.C. was discovered in the coastal city of Ugarit" in present-day Lebanon.

The Phoenicians were merchants, and so, in order to record their trading activities and keep records of their business transactions, they worked hard to combine characters that made sense to what they wanted to communicate. According to Caldwell and Gyles (1966):

The Phoenicians' chief gift to the west was the diffusion of the alphabet. The problem of its origin is obscure. The inscriptions found in a temple in the mining region of Sinai and dated variously between 1600 and 1500 B.C. furnish a possible prototype, but inscriptions from Byblos and other northern Syrian cities show a trend toward the development of alphabetic scripts, some from hieroglyphics and some from cuneiform antecedents.... It seems ... that the Phoenicians, influenced by Egyptian hieratic writing and by earlier attempts at simplifying writing in Syria, evolved a system of signs that represented individual consonants, vowel signs being a contribution from the Greeks. (p. 145)

By the close of the ninth century, the Phoenician alphabet had become common in Syria, and as a result of the frequent trading activities in the region, the Greeks adopted and transformed the Phoenician alphabet into that which is now being used in the Western world (Caldwell & Gyles, 1966).

THE EARLY SCHOOLS IN THE REGION

Ancient schools in the Middle East and North Africa were not organized as we see in our cities and towns and villages today. They were often organized in a temple or palace or in the open. The Sumerians set up their schools in temples. The schools were called *edubbas* or "tablet houses." In these schools, the students studied religion, reading and writing, botany, and arithmetic. The students trained to become scribes, the most noble of all the professions at the time.

The schools were intended for upper-class children, especially boys. In many cases, girls had very little access to schooling. The general argument was that it was not advisable to teach girls how to read or write (Heyworth-Dunne,

1938). Only the rich or upper-class citizens provided minimal education for their daughters. Many girls stayed at home and observed their mothers performing household chores.

Boys were expected to leave the home and work in the open fields to bring home food for the family. They were also encouraged to get employment outside the home. The most prestigious occupation at the time was to be a scribe, a job solely reserved for men.

Teachers in the ancient schools were essentially men. They were also religious leaders. There was therefore nothing like separation of church and state. Teachers were encouraged by parents to use the cane at all times when a student misbehaved. A teacher who did not frequently use the cane was considered to be weak or unfit to train children. Some indeed looked stern in the classroom. The prevailing psychology at the time was that effective learning took place only when the child was threatened with punishment.

Individual differences were not recognized in the classroom. All students were required to learn at the same pace. In ancient Egypt, students had to memorize all seven hundred letters in the alphabet, a task that often overwhelmed the students. Those who slacked were considered to be lazy and were never spared the rod.

The school day was long, and discipline was harsh. The students were afraid to break school rules because the teachers did not hesitate to use the whip for any school infraction. Below is a story of a schoolboy in Sumer. The story was copied on a tablet. It gives an account of the life of a student, Tolbi, who had a bad day in school.

A Bad Day at School

Before going to bed, a schoolboy called Tolbi asked the family servants to wake him in time for class. But they failed to wake him. Tolbi slept late. When he did awake, he jumped out of bed and quickly dressed. He grabbed two rolls for lunch and ran all the way to school. He was filled with fear as he entered the classroom and bowed low before his teacher.

His low bow did not save him from a terrible day, however. Things continued to go wrong. First, he had been late. Then later on in the day, he forgot some lines in the lesson he wrote on his tablet. Next, he talked to a friend in class without permission. "The man in charge of the whip" beat him for all these things and also for breaking other school rules. But the boy had a rich father who invited the poorly paid teacher to dinner. The father gave the teacher new clothes, a ring for his finger, and many other gifts. After this visit to the boy's home, the teacher began to treat his student more kindly. (Social Science Staff of the Educational Research Council of America, 1982, pp. 111–12)

Very few girls had the opportunity to attend school to become teachers. In the fifth century, an Egyptian woman, Hypatia, is believed to have taught philosophy and mathematics in Alexandria, Egypt.

Methods of teaching consisted of rote learning, copying, and recitation. Students had to develop sharp acumen to absorb information and produce it exactly as they had been told. Students spent long hours memorizing information from their teachers. Those who failed to reproduce information were whipped and given another opportunity to relearn it. As scribes, people were not expected to make mistakes in their presentations or recording of events, and so teachers were very strict on enforcing discipline, punctuality, and a high sense of responsibility.

Students started school at a tender age. In Egypt, many of the male students started school at the age of 4 or 5. In ancient Sumer, the age was the same. Students stayed in school until they mastered what they were supposed to know. The curriculum consisted essentially of reading, writing, and mathematics. Later, courses like poetry, music, art, and physical education were added to the curriculum.

The schooling activities in the Middle East and North Africa attracted the attention of the Greeks and other Europeans. Greek scholars such as Plato, Pythagoras, Lycurgus, and Solon studied in ancient Egypt (Johnson et al., 2005). All these scholars were great men whose influence on modern education is still felt in the region as well as all over the world. The philosophical ideas of Plato, for instance, are the bedrock of "idealism." Lycurgus, a great Greek statesman, has left an indelible mark in legal studies all over the Western world; Pythagoras is famous all over the world for his mathematical contributions, including the Pythagorean Theorem; and Solon in the sixth century B.C. studied Egyptian laws and later applied the Egyptian legal system in Athens.

THE LIBRARY AT ALEXANDRIA, EGYPT

To show his interest in learning, the Egyptian pharaoh Ptolemy I Soter established a library in Alexandria in 375 B.C. In this library were found all sorts classical works, including books and scrolls. Among them were the works of Plato and Aristotle; the original manuscripts of Sophocles; Egyptian works on medicine, astronomy, mathematics, chemistry, and physics; and several literary works from the ancient world. It is believed to have housed more than seven hundred scrolls and tablets. Scholars from all over the ancient world went and studied there. Students used this library to learn about the ancient world and to conduct research.

SUMMARY

Schooling in the Middle East and North Africa has a long tradition. It followed the invention of writing. Schooling became an important social institution because it helped ancient governments to organize their social, economic, and political activities. Unfortunately, only boys had the opportunity to attend school to become scribes, a profession that was highly regarded by the society. There was no separation of church and state. Parents cooperated with teachers to discipline stubborn students. The main method of teaching was rote learning.

The school day was long and hard. Teachers were quick to use the cane to correct student misbehavior. Slower learners often received harsher treatment from their teacher because they were considered to be lazy. Since very few girls had the opportunity to attend school, very few women, if any, in ancient societies had the chance to be teachers or scribes.

REFERENCES

Brewer, D. J., & Teeter, E. (1999). *Egypt and the Egyptians*. Cambridge: Cambridge University Press.

Caldwell, W. E., & Gyles, M. F. (1966). *The ancient world*. New York: Holt, Rinehart, & Winston.

Easton, S. C. (1964). *The heritage of the past: From the earliest times to 1500*. New York: Holt, Rinehart, & Winston.

Hartt, F. (1993). *Art: A history of painting, sculpture, architecture*. Englewood Cliffs, NJ: Prentice-Hall.

Hawkins, J. D. (1979). The origin and dissemination of writing in Western Asia. In M. P. R. S. Moorey (Ed.), *The origins of civilization: Wolfson College lectures, 1978*. Oxford, England: Clarendon.

Heyworth-Dunne, J. (1938). *An introduction to the history of education in modern Egypt*. London: Luzac.

Johnson, J. A., Dupuis, V. L., Musial, D., Hall, G. E., & Gollnick, D. M. (2005). *Introduction to the foundations of American education*. Boston: Allyn & Bacon.

Social Science Staff of the Educational Research Council of America. (1982). *The growth of civilization*. Boston: Allyn & Bacon.

Walker, J. (2003). *One hundred things you should know about ancient Egypt*. Essex, England: Barnes & Noble.

Webb, L. D., Metha, A., & Jordan, K. F. (2000). *Foundations of American education*. Columbus, OH: Prentice-Hall.

Williams, A. (1968). *Britain and France in the Middle East and North Africa, 1914–1967*. New York: St. Martin's.

Chapter 2

THE FOUNDATIONS OF MODERN EDUCATION IN THE MIDDLE EAST AND NORTH AFRICA

The people of North Africa and the Middle East have cherished schooling for more than two millennia now. As already pointed out, schools flourished in ancient Mesopotamia and Egypt. Their organization was, however, quite different from what we see today in our modern school system. The mode of instruction was essentially lecture and memorization. Students learned how to read, write, and compute numbers. The curriculum consisted of religion, mathematics, and reading. There were no special buildings constructed for the purpose of teaching and learning. A teacher's home, temple, or palace served as the classroom. Very few girls had the opportunity to attend any of these schools.

The introduction of Islam in the region brought into existence new forms of traditional schools—*kuttabs* and *madrasahs*. The kuttabs were traditional schools that emphasized the teaching of religion, specifically Islam. The medium of instruction was Arabic. The method of teaching was by and large memorization (Boyle, 2006). Students were required to memorize the entire Quran before graduating. These were nongraded schools. The kuttabs offered instruction mostly to male students. The students sat on a mat on the floor with no furniture and repeated after the teacher (*fqih*). While memorizing the text, the students moved the upper part of their bodies back and forth, at the same time saying aloud their portion of the Quran. To the outsider, the method of instruction and classroom management were chaotic, disorganized, and unorthodox. As Starrett (1995) has argued:

The lack of furniture and the children's occasional involvement in economic pursuit, such as plaiting straw mats for sale, tended to upset foreigners whose understanding of schooling required a specific interior architecture, trained and disinterested professionals, and the full uninterrupted attention of all parties. Visitors deprecated the unkept appearance of kuttabs and, interpreting their physical organization as the result mainly of poverty, appealed for their provision with symbols of modern learning such as textbooks and blackboards. (p. 955)

Because learning in the kuttabs consisted essentially of memorization, many observers believed that the students did not always understand what they were taught. "Learning to recite verses of the Koran without any possible comprehension of its contents was an exercise that, from an educational viewpoint, although possibly not from a religious one, cannot be considered as particularly productive" (Szyliowicz, 1971, p. 58).

In the classroom, teachers had absolute control over what students learned. They possessed much authority and determined appropriate punishment for school infractions such as the use of bad language and manners.

The education of girls did not receive serious attention. It was provided in a different format. Girls were generally considered to be academically inferior to boys, and so their education was less rigorous. This was an ancient idea that was carried into modern times. The argument was that teaching a girl reading and writing skills was like imposing severe mental torture on her. There was a popular saying that a woman who was taught how to read and write was like a serpent that had drunk poison.

Kuttab teachers were expected to lead honest and "holy" lives, know the Quran by heart, and be trustworthy. They were not respected by the public, however, chiefly because they received meager remuneration. People often compared their social status to bloodletters or weavers. As Szyliowicz (1971) has suggested:

One reason for this attitude may have been that teachers were generally regarded as being rather stupid. And it is true that most were quite ignorant, the ability to read the Koran and to explain its contents in a simple manner sufficing to qualify a prospective teacher. (p. 55)

The main curriculum was focused on the Holy Quran. Students learned pages upon pages from the Quran daily. The main philosophy behind this new form of schooling was to inculcate in the students fear and respect for their Maker and society. Teachers had the power to determine the pace of instruction, mode of learning, and rate of learning and, above all, to punish failing students (Totah, 1926). Totah (1926) notes that teachers received their payments "in the form of chickens, eggs, milk, bread, and vegetables" (p. 35).

Parents had little or no role in what students learned at school. The schools were usually located in the mosque or a building attached to the mosques or courts of kings or rulers. Other schools were located in the homes of people, especially teachers. The students sat on the floor and listened to their instructor (*Ulama*).

These schools were distributed all over the region. Totah (1926) provides a few examples (see table 2.1).

It is clear from the table that Cairo, Damascus, and Baghdad had most schools at the time. Alexandria—once the greatest city of the ancient world, a great center for learning during the Middle Ages, and famous for its library

Table 2.1
Distribution of Schools (Selected Locations) in the Middle East and North
Africa before the Introduction of Modern Schools

City	Number
Aleppo	14
Baghdad	40
Cairo	74
Damascus	73
Damietta	1
Dinaisir	1
Granada	1
Hama	3
Homs	1
Jerusalem	41
Maknassah	3
Mecca	1
Mosul	9
Nisibin (Nisibis)	2
Al-Raha (Edessa)	1
Rās al-'Ain	1
Tripoli (Syria)	13
Wāsit	1

Source: Totah, 1926, p. 23.

and education—had a similar number of schools to Cairo, Damascus, or Baghdad. However the destruction of the city during the civil war that occurred
under the Roman emperor Aurelian in the late third century A.D. makes it hard
to determine the exact number of schools.

Madrasahs were organized for adolescents, and they functioned like secondary
or high schools. Some of the students wore beards. The classroom structure was
like that of the kuttabs, but the curriculum for the madrasahs was broader than
the kuttabs'. It included lessons on Islamic law, logic, mathematics, geometry,
astronomy, music, the natural sciences, medicine, literature, rhetoric, and grammar. Here again, the lecture method was the main mode of instruction. Teachers
had absolute control over what to teach and how to teach it. The reputation of
teachers and the facilities in the madrasahs played a significant role in attracting
students to these schools. Madrasahs, like kuttabs, were organized in mosques.
These served as colleges and produced leaders for the Islamic communities.

THE OTTOMAN EMPIRE AND EDUCATION IN MIDDLE EAST AND NORTH AFRICA

The Ottoman Empire played a significant role in modernizing education in
the region (Anderson, 1984). Observing the educational progress in Egypt and

other areas in the region, it dawned on the Ottoman sultan that if the empire were to withstand the winds of change that were blowing, reforms in the state administration and organization were necessary. The Ottoman ruler, Salem III, looked to Europe for help in modernizing the educational system in the empire. France was the final destination that the emperor looked for help. French missionaries entered the Ottoman Empire and the Middle East, especially the Holy Land, Syria, Lebanon, and North Africa, in the 1850s to help modernize the educational system in the region. Burrows (1986) has clearly pointed out

that Catholicism tends to rely on a whole panoply of various orders for its proselytism. The number who eventually opened up missions in the Middle East was indeed large, but as with French mission this was a process that took place after 1860. In the *mémoire* written by Varenne in 1825 about Lazarists, the secretary to the French embassy in Constantinople noted that the Carmelites only had two missionaries in the whole Middle East, the Cordeliers five; the Dominicans also a relatively small number as they only had the parish of Saint-Pierre-de-Galata under their care. (p. 115–16)

To a vary large extent, the French missionaries were accepted in the Middle East and North Africa because they fulfilled a need that indigenous people could not satisfy and were also seen as not trying to convert the Muslims to Christianity. This was essential, because Islam had at that time taken root in the region. Any attempt to supplant the Islamic religion with the Christian religion would have angered the local inhabitants.

With the help of France, the Ottoman emperor modernized the educational system within the empire, which at that time included most of the countries in the Middle East and North Africa. As part of the modernization process, the emperor sent students to Europe, particularly France, to learn modern methods of administration, political economy, and military organization.

As Szyliowicz (1971) has argued:

The opening of these schools, however, must be viewed as a truly innovative breakthrough in the creation of a modern educational system for the Empire. For the first time in Ottoman history, secular public schools had been established, and control of the education was no longer the sole responsibility of the *ulema* but was vested in a Council of Public Instruction, the forerunner of the Ministry of Education. This was an important step toward the creation of an integrated secular system. (p. 141)

Later, as the years passed by, the emperor published what was known as the Regulation of General Education in 1869. In this document, the government made clear the educational expectations for all citizens within the empire. The main provisions included the following:

1. Elementary education would be free.
2. Tuition in every secondary school would be free.
3. Every major village was to get an elementary school.

4. The provision of secondary education was to be the responsibility of each governor.
5. The government was to be responsible for the provision of university education.
6. Teacher training institutions were to be developed.
7. Teaching methods were to be reformed, and the procedure for teacher promotion modified, to help boost morale of teachers.

The implementation of these policies rapidly increased school enrollments for both boys and girls. Altogether, 242,017 boys and 126,459 girls enrolled in the schools throughout the Empire (Szyliowicz, 1973). This was an important development because the education of girls had for many years been frowned upon by tradition and custom throughout the region. Even in the traditional schools, girls had very limited access to the curriculum and education in general. Certain sections of the Quran were out of bounds to girls at school, particularly the "Surat Yusuf" (Heyworth-Dunne, 1938).

The French government, which acted as the catalyst for the educational changes, promoted the education of girls, and it was no wonder that the sultan of the Ottoman Empire paid greater attention to the education of girls at this time, when other nations in the region paid little or no attention to girls' education.

One of the important developments in the development of modern education in the Middle East and North Africa was the introduction of several new forms of schools. The Galatasaray Lycée established in Turkey was modeled along the lines of the schools in France. Its curriculum consisted of history, geography, mathematics, science, drawing, calligraphy, Latin, Persian, and French. French was the language of instruction, and this was deliberately done to promote French culture and values in the region.

Another type of modern school introduced in the Ottoman Empire was the Mülkiye. This was an institution that catered for the educational needs of the upper-class students. These institutions were also mainly found in the urban centers. The Mülkiye prepared students for high government positions. The curriculum was essentially like the one designed for the Galatasaray Lycée. The only difference was that the Mülkiye was established to produce personnel to administer affairs within the Ottoman Empire (Szyliowicz, 1971).

The Harbiye, a military academy opened in the mid-nineteenth century, also set the tone for educational reforms and modernization. The Harbiye produced top-class military officers and personnel who gave the army a new image throughout the Empire (Mizikaci, 2006).

Many of the teachers in these modern schools were Europeans because there was shortage of teachers in the Empire. Very few people could read and write, and so in order to accelerate the pace of educational reforms, the sultan found it necessary to recruit teachers from outside the Empire. The textbooks used were also of European origin. The curriculum contained European topics and ideas because at this time local textbooks had not been produced to meet the needs of the educational reformers.

To solve the problem of the teacher shortage, the government sent many educated people abroad for further studies. This practice marked the beginning of international education in the region. When the students returned to the Empire, they were either sent to teach or to work at a location where people with modern skills were required.

To solve the problem of textbooks, the government launched an intensive program to translate the European textbooks into local languages. These were translated and published by the schools themselves. It was not an easy task, but with the assistance of numerous Europeans, the job was done to meet the needs of the Ottomans.

THE FRENCH IN NORTH AFRICA

The French were also very active in modernizing the schools in Algeria. Until the involvement of the French in the development of education on Algeria, Muslims had established Islamic schools, kuttabs, and madrasahs. These schools provided the students with the essential skills all Muslims were expected to acquire. The schools taught the students how to pray, recitation of the Quran by heart, and the correct movements that accompanied prayers. Above all, the Muslim schools prepared children to be good citizens in "accordance with Moslem ethics" and made them "part of the religious system which controlled almost every act of life" (Heyworth-Dunne, 1938, p. 6).

With this as the background, the French had initial problems regarding what the new schools should teach or whose curriculum was to be used. Muslims had fought hard in the past to occupy Algeria, and so there were no easy answers to these questions.

In order to avoid any major confrontation with the Muslim community, the French extended modern schools to the local Berber community. The Berbers were not Arabs, and the French took advantage of that fact to extend schools to them, hoping to win their support and sympathy in the country. However, this did not work very well because most of the Berbers had embraced the Islamic faith and were not prepared to convert to Christianity. The Berbers therefore decided to side with the Arabs in resisting French schools and religious ideas (Courtney-Clark, 1996).

The French Policy of Assimilation and Educational Expansion in Algeria

The French policy of assimilation formed the basis for developing schools in Algeria and other French colonies. This policy made Algeria an "extension of France," not a colony. The implication was that the quality of schools that the French wanted to establish in Algeria and other areas in North Africa were to be similar to those in France. This meant that expensive schools were to be developed in Algeria, as well as in other French colonies in the region such as

Tunisia and Morocco (Kinsey, 1971). Admission to the schools was open to all, including both Muslims and Christians.

It is generally argued that the French efforts at educational development in Algeria left much to be desired. In the words of Heggoy (1973):

Up to 1914, French efforts to educate Algerian children seemed inadequate. In 1907, for example, there were only 33,000 young Muslims, mostly boys, in official schools. Not until 1917 was any attempt made to make primary education compulsory for boys, and then the law applied only to children living within three kilometers of a regularly established "native" ... public school.... Urban children always had better opportunities to attend schools. Besides the creation of schools for the sons of notables decreed by Napoleon III, the first official notice of native public education came in 1892. The law dealt with special education, that is, with a program inferior to that offered in France itself and to European settlers in Algeria. (p. 185–86)

To a very great extent, the beneficiaries of French school systems were Europeans. They included children from Spain, Italy, and France and of Algerian Jews (Balch, 1909). In point of fact, the French had no inclination of enforcing French religious practices on the Muslim children in Algeria. The policy was to leave them alone if they wanted to be so, but to embrace them if they decided to accept French values and religious and educational practices. Very few Muslim children, especially girls, therefore enrolled in the French schools (Balch, 1909). In order to entice more Muslims into the French way of life, in 1850, the French government set up three Muslim schools (madrasahs) "to prepare functionaries for the Islamic cult and for Muslim courts" (Heggoy & Zingg, 1976, p. 572). In these schools, Arabic and French were used as the media of instruction.

Educational Reforms in Morocco

In Morocco, the French were very active. They laid the foundations of modern education in the country. Here again, the French had to confront Islam and Muslims in the quest to introduce a modern form of schooling. The Islamic religion was strong in Morocco at the time, and the local people had set up their Islamic schools (kuttabs and madrasahs), where the Quran formed the main basis for instruction and school organization. Here again, Muslims resisted the French form of schooling. Most of the beneficiaries of the French schools were Europeans and Moroccan Jews. Muslims resisted French schooling to such an extent that by 1954 only 12 percent of Muslim children were in public schools "in spite of the efforts made by the French during the last years of protectorate" (Hourani, 2002, p. 390).

Educational Reforms in Syria

Syria also had assistance from France in modernizing education after the collapse of the Ottoman Empire after World War I. As in the other countries in the

Table 2.2
Weekly Distribution of Hours* in Senior High School, Northern Region, United Arab Republic (Syria)

Subjects	First Year	Second Year** Literary	Second Year** Science	Third Year Literary	Third Year Science
Religious education	2	2	2	2	2
Arabic language and literature	7	7	5	7	5
Foreign language (English or French)	6	7	5	7	5
Mathematics	4	2	6	2	6
History	2	3	1	3	1
Geography	2	3	1	3	1
Philosophy and social studies	1	3	1	3	1
Physics	2	2	3	2	3
Chemistry	2		3		3
Natural history	2	1	3	1	3
Music	1	1	1	1	1
Art	1	1	1	1	1
Physical education	2	2	2	2	2
Military training	2	2	2	2	2
Weekly load	*36*	*36*	*36*	*36*	*36*

* Class hour = 50 minutes
** Choice of literary or scientific course is made in grade 11

Source: Potter, 1961, p. 36.

region, however, Syria did not like the educational system promoted by the French. It had to wait to be independent before developing its own educational system. The new education system in Syria followed much the same system developed in Egypt by the British following the formation in 1958 of the United Arab Republic between Egypt and Syria. Table 2.2 shows a typical timetable used in a high school in Syria during the early part of the modernization process.

MOHAMMAD ALI AND EDUCATIONAL REFORMS IN EGYPT

Between 1809 and 1844, the Egyptian government under Mohammad Ali, in an effort to modernize the educational system in Egypt, sent several students abroad to study various courses such as mathematics, agriculture, medicine, and administration. In 1809, about twenty-eight students were abroad to study in the new education institutions that were springing up all over Europe. Most of the students were sent to France or England. In 1826, the Egyptian government under Mohammad Ali sent forty-four students to countries such as France, England, Spain, and Italy to study. They stayed in Europe from one to nine years, depending upon the duration of the program in which the students were enrolled. Those who studied medicine stayed longer than those who studied liberal arts such as education, who spent a few years abroad. The courses the students studied included, but were not limited to:

- Agriculture
- Civil administration
- Military administration
- Naval administration
- Diplomacy
- Hydraulics
- Mechanics
- Artillery
- Metal-founding and arms-making
- Printing
- Lithography and engraving
- Chemistry
- Medicine—surgery, anatomy, physiology, and hygiene
- Agriculture
- Translation
- Natural history
- Mining

(Heyworth-Dunne, 1938, pp. 159–63)

Of the forty-four students who went to study abroad in 1826, all were boys. They were selected from all parts of the country. Some were Muslims and some Christians. Their ages ranged between 15 and 38.

In 1816, Mohammad Ali's government opened the first modern school in the country. The school opened with eighty students. Each student was given a monthly allowance and was clothed and fed free of charge (Heyworth-Dunne, 1938). The Egyptian government imported surveying, mathematical, and astronomical equipment from England. Teachers were brought from Constantinople to teach in the school.

Some of the teachers in the school were "Christian priests, even for teaching Arabic" (Heyworth-Dunne, 1938, p. 110), an experiment that was risky but worked out for Mohammad Ali. His main goal was to look for the best teachers of the day for his new schools, and so he did not worry about the religious inclinations of the people who worked in the schools.

The students studied most of the day in the classroom. Classes started early in the morning and ended late in the evening. The idea was to help the students spend quality time in the classroom with their teachers. They studied numerous courses such as religion, reading, mathematics, writing, and foreign languages, including Turkish, Persian, and Italian. The government wanted the new schools to equip students with essential skills that would help Egypt modernize the administration of the country.

Apart from the elementary schools, the Egyptian government established some tertiary institutions that were designed to provide manpower for the various sectors of the economy. Some of these were established to take care of the health and welfare needs of the people. These new institutions included medical schools, a pharmacy school, military schools, a veterinary school, and a music school. In order to promote efficiency in government administration, the Egyptians decided to expand the types of educational institutions in the country. Hence the government

established a school of accounting (1826), civil school (1829), and a school of administration (1834). To provide manpower for his industrial and agricultural enterprises, he [Mohammed Ali] opened an industrial school and a school of irrigation in 1831 and a school of agriculture three years later.... This early attempt at relating education functionally to the perceived manpower needs of the society served above all to emphasize the need for coordinated educational planning among the various parts of an educational system and the complex problems involved in attempting to establish modern institutions in a traditional setting. (Szyliowicz, 1971, p. 103)

The curriculum in these schools included biology, chemistry, physics, geometry, reading, and, of course, religion. The medium of instruction was either French or English. Arabic was also used, but since most of the teachers were Europeans who could not speak or read Arabic, this had limited use in the schools. Courses that attracted the attention of the government included pharmacy, engineering, signals, and music.

The new schools that Mohammad Ali set up were open to all, including females. However, at that time very few females enrolled in the schools because public opinion was very much against the idea of girls studying in schools (Heyworth-Dunne, 1938). It was in 1873 that the Egyptian government opened the country's first school for girls. These schools were in the urban centers such as Alexandria and Cairo.

The Educational Law of 1867 introduced some significant provisions in the development of education in Egypt. It contained forty clauses that laid down guidelines for school organization and administration. Among other things, the 1867 law stated that:

1. Students were to attend school of their own free will; promotion of students was to be based upon performance of the annual examination.
2. Teachers had to live according to a high moral standard of respectability. They must know the Quran and their religion thoroughly, should have beautiful calligraphy, and must know arithmetic.
3. Students who had been recommended for good conduct were to receive free uniforms from the state.
4. The books to be used in the schools were to be prescribed by the government.
5. The school furniture was to consist of a chair for the teacher and benches for students in the larger schools or mats for elementary schools.

6. Students suffering from serious or contagious illness were not to be allowed admission to the schools.
7. Schools were to be inspected by health officials.
8. Essentially, local people were to pay for furniture.
9. Dormitory furniture, food, clothing, and students' materials were to be paid for from special funds; where the funds were not sufficient, local people had to pay the difference.
10. Students were to be accepted in the schools irrespective of their religious beliefs.
11. Uniforms were to be worn on all occasions and to consist of special designs issued by the government. A student was to be issued three shirts, three pairs of drawers, three belts, three tunics, three waistcoats, three skullcaps, four pairs of white stockings, and a winter coat every two years.
12. A ceremony was to be held at the end of the academic year to honor students. A military band was to be in attendance to provide music for the occasion.
13. Orphans and poor children could be admitted gratuitously.
14. The syllabus was to include:

    • Arabic grammar, reading, and ethics
    • A modern European language, Turkish, or another language, which the student was to learn to read, write, and translate
    • Elementary geography and ancient history
    • Elementary arithmetic, commercial knowledge, linear drawing, and geometry
    • Zoology, botany, and principles of agriculture
    • Drawing and calligraphy

It was against this background that the British took over the educational affairs of the country in 1882. Between 1882 and 1922, the British created an educational system that greatly changed the pattern of schooling in Egypt (Langhor, 2005).

BRITAIN AND THE MODERNIZATION OF SCHOOLS IN EGYPT, 1882–1922

Great Britain, like France, was very instrumental in laying the foundations of modern education in the Middle East and North Africa. The British worked in many areas of the region, including Egypt, Syria, and Lebanon. In Egypt, the British made some progress in modernizing education under the leadership of Lord Cramer. He adopted a conservative approach to the development of education in the country, in the sense that he did not want schooling to be open to all in society. His policy was that schooling should be limited to people who had the ability to pay fees to support themselves. To this end, he did not make education free for all. He expected students to pay fees and to take and pass examinations before being promoted to the next grade.

Many students could not master the English language before sitting for examinations and so the school dropout rate was very high. Examinations, syllabi, timetables, and teaching, teacher recruitment, and training were all in the hands of the British. The Department of Public Instruction was set up to be responsible for education. This department decided what was to be taught at school and what was not to be taught (Langhor, 2005). The prescriptions from the department were generally programs that promoted British interests in the country and not those of the local people. The schools were so rigidly controlled that, in the words of Szyliowicz (1971), learning became "a stultifying experience" (p. 125). Arabic and Islamic studies did not benefit very much from the British educational system.

It was also not the policy of the British government to provide higher education in the country. The main goal of the British education policy was to produce lower-level personnel to help the British administration. Parents who wanted higher education for their children had to find it abroad. The medium of instruction in all the schools was English. French and Arabic did not receive any serious attention, even though these were the languages that were used by most of the students. The use of English in many cases made learning difficult for many of the students.

The curriculum for secondary education was determined by the British colonial government, and it was similar to that in use in England. Reid (1983) has identified a typical history syllabus that was often used in Egyptian secondary schools:

The Awakening of Learning in Europe
The Expansion and Spread of Western Nations
The Main Events of the 17th and 18th Centuries in France, Russia, and Prussia
The War of the Austrian Succession; the Seven Years' War
Europe in the 19th Century; the French Revolution; the Congress of Vienna
The History of Rome
Introduction to the Political Sciences, primarily the formation of institutions in England and France
Principles of Political Science and Institutional History
The History of Government Organization
Feudalism in France, England, and Germany
The Progress and Influence of English Institutions
The Growth of Royal Power in France, the French Revolution
Introduction to Government Institutions in England, Turkey, France, the U.S., Germany, and Russia (p. 384)

Of course, such a course of study did not meet the aspirations of the students. There was nothing on the syllabus that made reference to the needs and values of the students. Although there were many things about Egypt that the teachers could have included in the curriculum, the British school administrators ignored local history and geography because their main objective was to change the way of life of the local people as the British had done elsewhere in Asia and Africa (Thompson, 1981).

The British promoted extracurricular activities in all the schools they established or supported. The most popular was soccer. In the sports arena, religion and social classes had no place. All the students played together on the same team for their institutions. No emphasis was placed on religion when selecting activities or players for games.

The education of girls received a boost under the colonial administration. The British did not believe that it was wrong to teach girls how to read and write or even to study certain subjects such as mathematics or science. Girls in England at that time were studying all sorts courses offered at school. Accordingly, the British expanded the curriculum for girls to include mathematics, science, and hygiene, although traditional women's courses such as sewing and needlework remained in the curriculum (Russell, 2002).

Although the British made strenuous efforts and in a few cases attempted to overlook tradition in the education of girls, there were nevertheless clear distinctions between the schooling for girls and boys. The aim for girls' education was to prepare them for the home, while the aim of schooling for boys was to prepare them for the world of work. With this as the backdrop, the education of girls consisted more of courses that were designed to produce women who would be competent mothers for children and wives for men. For instance, the students used a hygiene book entitled *Hygiene for Elementary Schools*, written by Dr. Sarubyaq. The textbook had two versions, one for boys and the other for girls. The girls' edition contained fifty more pages because in it the author put more emphasis on "clothing, sleep, housing, child-care, first aid, and home nursing" (Russell, 2002, p. 52).

In the United Arab Emirates, the British were the first to build modern schools. The first of these opened in Sharjah in 1953. Later, they set up the first primary school for girls in the same city. A separate school for girls was necessary because of the differential attitude of some parents toward the education of boys and girls. The other places in the Emirates where the British actively helped to establish modern schools were Abu Dhabi, Ras al Khaymah, and Khawr Fakkan. They introduced comprehensive curricula in these schools, which were set up like the British models. The curriculum in these schools included English, mathematics, music, physical education, Arabic, and art.

Missionaries from France, Britain, and the United States also had significant impact on the development of modern education in North Africa and the Middle East. The activities of the foreign missionaries were very effective and common in the Levant. Catholic missionaries, particularly the Jesuits and the Lazarists, established schools in Lebanon, Syria, and other locations in the region. The Jesuits established the first modern school in Ayn-Tura, Syria, in 1734 and a boys' school in Damascus in 1755. In 1848 they founded another at Ghazir. This institution later became known as the University of St. Joseph. The missionaries also paid attention to the education of girls and in 1846 opened a school for girls in Beirut.

American missionaries set up schools in Jerusalem, Beirut, and other places such as Tripoli, Lebanon. In 1866, the American missionaries working in the area founded the Syrian Protestant College, which in 1920 became known as the American University of Beirut (AUB). The Americans, like their French counterparts, showed an interest in developing elementary and high school education.

Muslims did not for a moment neglect education for children in the region. They continued to set up schools for both boys and girls throughout the region.

This was done to meet the rising need of the people, especially girls, to attend school. Muslims competed with Christians in the establishment and development of schools in both urban and rural areas. Like the Christians, Muslims had schools in places like Aleppo, Jerusalem, Beirut, Nablus, and Homs (see table 2.3).

FOUNDATIONS OF EDUCATION IN ISRAEL

Until the establishment of the State of Israel in 1948 there were several Jewish communities scattered throughout Palestine. Some Jewish parents sent their sons to the kuttabs, where they studied Arabic or Ladino (Kurian, 1988). Another type of religious school was the Heder, which existed in the region to promote Jewish philosophy, tradition, and culture. The language of instruction in the heder was Yiddish, the language spoken by the Jews.

The development of a modern school system in Israel started in the late 1850s when a group of Jews founded a school in Jerusalem. A second school was established exclusively for girls in 1870. Both schools were created to provide education that would cater to the needs of Jewish children.

In 1948, the United Nations voted to establish a home in Palestine for Jews who were scattered around the world. Jewish immigrants from nearly eighty countries across the world later made the new state their home. Most of the immigrants in the new state came from Austria, Britain, Egypt, Ethiopia, France, Italy, Morocco, Poland, Russia, and Tunisia. Some of these immigrants were Jews, Arabs, Druze, and Circassian (Israel, 1996).

The one thing that could unite these immigrants as a nation was an education system that would give them a common identity. The Israeli government and religious groups set up schools that put emphasis on creating a common identity for all the citizens in the new nation. In the curriculum that the schools followed the study of Hebrew was emphasized, although other languages such as Arabic, English, and French were also taught. The Bible, Talmud, and Quran, were all used in the schools to provide religious education for the new immigrants.

Types of Schools in Israel

There are four types of schools in Israel:

- State schools
- State religious schools
- Arab and Druze schools
- Independent private schools. (Jewish Agency for Israel, 2008)

State Schools

As the name implies, state schools are organized under the auspices of the government. State schools exist to provide the government the opportunity to implement educational programs that give the state its identity. The basic

Table 2.3
The Distribution of Christian and Moslem Schools in Middle East and North Africa, 1882

	Christian Schools					Muslim Schools			
Locality	Boys	Girls	Percent*	Total	Percent**	Boys	Girls	Percent***	Total
Urban Localities									
Hasbayya	238	140	37	378	84	70	-	-	70
Jerusalem	861	926	52	1,787	83	360	-	-	360
Aleppo	1,205	810	40	2,015	79	550	-	-	550
Beirut	4,361	5,029	54	9,390	78	2,170	452	17	2,622
			Average 63 percent of students in urban Christian schools.						
Akka	250	150[y]	38+	400[y]	62+	250	-	-	250
al-Salt	165[yy]	70[yy]	30	235	57	180	-	-	180
Sayda	267	180	40	447	53	330	60	15	390
Tripoli + Mina	265	355	57	620	47	553	160	22	713
Lataqiyya	164	160	49	324	39	500	-	-	500
Horns	420	190	31	610	27	1,690	-	-	1,690
Nablus	95	42	31	137	11	986	100	9	1,086
Hama	70	20	22	90	8	1,085	-	-	1,085
Rural Areas									
ᶜAjlun + Balqaʾ	300	150	33	450	67	220	-	-	220
Hawran excl. ᶜAjlun	550	-	-	550	48	600	-	-	600
Marj ᶜUyun	595	180	23	775	34	1,000	500	33	1,500

* Percent girls among students in Christian schools in the locality/area.
** Percent students in Christian schools among students in the locality.
*** Percent girls among students in Muslim schools in the locality.
[y] The number of girl students in the girl school of the Benevolent Litarary Society is not known.
[yy] In the CMS school there are "95 pupils, both boys and girls." They have been assumed to be 45 boys and 50 girls.

Source: Diab & Wåhlin, 1950, p. 113.

curriculum includes Jewish studies, mathematics, science, and tradition and observance. Admission is open to all children, irrespective of religion, race, or gender.

State schools are administered by the state and local committees. By getting involved in the administration of state schools, parents in the communities are able to add content that is of interest to them to the curriculum of state schools. This is particularly the case with Tali schools. Tali is a Hebrew acronym for "enriched Jewish studies." These Tali schools teach students issues concerning Jewish philosophy, culture, values, and tradition. State schools enroll more students than the other types of schools in Israel.

State Religious Schools

State religious schools provide opportunities for the state to infuse religious ideas into the school curriculum. These schools do not adhere to the principle of "separation of church and state" as seen in the public schools in the United States and other countries in western Europe. The curriculum is similar to that of the state schools. The only major difference is that the Torah (the five books of Moses—Genesis, Exodus, Leviticus, Numbers, and Deuteronomy) is used as the focus for instruction.

Arab and Druze Schools

These schools are organized for the Arab and Druze populations in Israel. They teach Arab and Hebrew languages, Arab, Jewish, and Druze history, and religion and culture. The Negev Bedouins fall under the Arab and Druze education system. The Druze are an Arab-speaking minority group in Israel, who have much in common with Arabs and Jews. The core curriculum used in the Arab and Druze schools includes subjects that all Israeli citizens are expected to know. The curriculum is designed to integrate Israeli immigrants into mainstream society.

Independent Religious Schools

The organization and administration of independent religious schools rests on the Talmud—the holy book of the Jewish faith. The emphasis in these schools is on religious education, although science, mathematics, and language skills are also taught. The schools are supported by the state and the Ministry of Education is not responsible for the curriculum used in these schools. The curriculum is designed by local communities to offer their children education that is fully immersed in Jewish religious ideas, tradition, and custom.

Independent Private Schools

These are private schools that seek approval from the Ministry of Education before enrolling students. Private schools may be religious or secular, or run by a foreign nation. These schools utilize state-mandated curricula; however, parents and teachers determine the instructional strategies and school norms, and the rules and policies that are deemed appropriate to promote efficiency in the administration and organization of the schools (Elazar, 1990; Ministry of Immigrant Absorption, 2005).

Despite the differences in the philosophies guiding each type of school, all the schools use a common core curriculum prescribed by the Ministry of Education, which is responsible for the education of all children.

Like other MENA countries, Britain, France, and the United States have all made significant contributions toward the development of schools in Israel. Individuals and groups from these countries also established schools in Israel during its formative years. In 1958, the United States established a private coeducational school, the Walworth Barbour American International School, in Even Yehuda, to provide education for American and other children in Israel (American International School, 2007).

SUMMARY

The process of modernizing education in the Middle East and North Africa had a gradual beginning. Until contact with the West was established, the main form of schooling for children were the kuttabs and madrasahs, schools that taught and promoted Islamic religion, values, and culture. The schools also encouraged reading and writing. These schools evolved from local initiatives.

The kuttabs and madrasahs were essentially meant for the education of boys. Very few girls had the opportunity to study in them. The emergence of Europeans, especially France and Britain, in the region changed the social dynamics of the schools.

Another important development that took place during this time was international education. The Ottoman Turks started this tradition of inviting Europeans to help in the modernization of education in the empire. Later, this policy was followed in Egypt and other places as more and more of the countries in the region became determined to establish schools that would help produce personnel for a modern society.

Europeans who worked in the region gave support to the education of girls and set up separate schools to teach them. Again, tradition did not favor coeducation, so the best way the Europeans could promote the education of girls while respecting local custom and tradition was to avoid teaching boys and girls together in the same classroom, especially adolescents (Trial & Bayly, 1950; Metz, 1992). Both boys and girls were often educated in boarding schools, although boarding schools were fewer than day schools because of the heavy financial responsibilities that go with their development and organization.

By 1875, both Christians and Muslims were promoting the education of girls. Christians had even established coeducational institutions in several of the large cities and towns. Admission was open to all students, regardless of their religion or place of birth.

REFERENCES

American International School. (2007). *High school profile-2007–2008*. Even Yehuda, Israel.

Anderson, L. (1984). Nineteenth-century reform in Ottoman Libya. *International Journal of Middle Eastern Studies, 16*(3), 325–48.

Balch, T. W. (1909). French colonization in North Africa. *American Political Science Review, 3*(4), 539–51.

Boyle, H. N. (2006). Memorization and learning in Islamic schools. *Comparative Education Review, 50*(3), 478–95.

Burrows, M. (1986). "Mission civilisatrice": French cultural policy in the Middle East, 1860–1914. *Historical Journal, 29*(1), 109–35.

Courtney-Clark, M. (1996). *Imazighen: The vanishing traditions of the Berber women*. New York: Clarkson Potter.

Diab, H., & Wåhlin, L. (1950). The geography of education in Syria in 1882. With a translation of "Education in Syria" by Shahin Makarius, 1883. *Geografisker Annaler*, series B. *Human Geography, 65*(2), 105–28.

Elazar, D. J. (1990). *Israel's education system: An introduction to a study program*. Jerusalem: Institute for the Study of Educational Systems.

Heggoy, A. A. (1973). Education in French Algeria: An essay on cultural conflict. *Comparative Education Review, 17*(2), 180–97.

Heggoy, A. A., & Zingg, P. J. (1976). French education in revolutionary North Africa. *International Journal of Middle East Studies, 7*(4), 571–78.

Heyworth-Dunne, J. (1938). *An introduction to the history of education in modern Egypt*. London: Luzac.

Hourani, A. (2002). *A history of the Arab peoples*. Cambridge, MA: Harvard University Press.

Israel National report. (1996). Report presented to the 45th session of the International conference on Education, Geneva, September 30–October 5. Available at http://www.ibe.unesco.org/countries/countryDossier/natrep96/israel96.pdf.

Jewish Agency for Israel. (2008). The ABC's of education in Israel, part 1. Available from http://www.jewishagency.org/JewishAgency/English/Aliyah/Aliyah+Info/Thoughts+on+Aliyah+and+Israel/Articles+about+Israel/Education+in+Israel++part+1.htm.

Kinsey, D. C. (1971). Efforts for educational synthesis under colonial rule: Egypt and Tunisia. *Comparative Education Review, 15*(2), 172–87.

Kurian, G. T. (1988). *World education encyclopedia*, vol. 2. pp. 636–47.

Langhor, V. (2005). Colonial educational systems and the spread of local religious movements: The cases of British Egypt and Punjab. *Society for Comparative Study of Society and History, 47*, 161–89.

Metz, H. D. (Ed.). (1992). *Saudi Arabia: A country study*. Washington, DC: GPO.

Ministry of Immigrant Absorption, (2005). *Education*. Author.

Mizikaci, F. (2006). *Higher education in Turkey*. UNESCO-CEPES Monographs on Higher Education. Bucharest, Romania: UNESCO European Center for Higher Education.

Potter, W. N. (1961). Modern education in Syria. *Comparative Education Review, 5*(1), 35–38.

Reid, D. M. (1983). Turn-of-the-century Egyptian school days. *Comparative Education Review, 27*(3), 374–93.

Russell, M. (2002). Competing, overlapping, and contradictory agendas: Egyptian education under British occupation, 1882–1922. *Comparative Studies of South Asia, Africa and the Middle East, 21*(1–2), 50–60.

Starrett, G. (1995). The hexis of interpretation: Islam and the body in the Egyptian popular school. *American Ethnologist, 22*(4), 953–69.

Szyliowicz, J. S. (1971). Elite recruitment in Turkey: The role of the Mulkiye. *World Politics, 23*(3), 371–98.

———. (1973). *Education and modernization in the Middle East.* Ithaca, NY: Cornell University Press.

Thompson, A. R. (1981). *Education and development in Africa.* New York: St. Martin's.

Totah, K. A. (1926). *The contribution of the Arabs to education.* New York: Teachers College Press.

Trial, G. T., & Bayly, W. (1950). Modern education in Saudi Arabia. *History of Education Journal, 1*(3), 121–33.

Chapter 3

INNOVATIONS IN THE CURRICULUM

The provision of education in the Middle East and North Africa (MENA) is the responsibility of the individual governments. Each country assumed full responsibility for the provision of education soon after independence (Qubain, 1966). This action was taken in order to include in the school curriculum items and issues that had a bearing on local interests, values, and cultural practices and aspirations. To this end, each country set up a ministry of education to formulate guidelines and oversee the development and implementation of curriculum. All public educational institutions in the region therefore are controlled by their respective governments, through the respective Ministry of Education. Private educational institutions also derive their authority to operate in the region through the Ministry of Education.

Although most of the countries in the region are held together by their religion and cultural practices, educational institutions in the Middle East and North Africa use different curriculum design and mapping strategies. In the countries where Islam is the dominant religion, the core curriculum for all public education institutions is based upon religion, namely, the Quran (Qubain, 1966). Thus in countries such as Egypt, Saudi Arabia, Libya, Jordan, Tunisia, Morocco, and Algeria, the Quran forms the basis of the core curriculum. In countries where Islam is not the predominant religion, the curriculum is not based upon the Quran. In Israel, the Torah is used in the schools for religious education.

The variety of schools available gives students the opportunity to study new courses in different schools without stepping out of the region. Students who wish to study the English language, for instance, do not have to leave their country to do so. There is an English school in all the countries in the Middle East and North Africa. Libya in 1980 forbade the teaching and learning of English in the country, but conditions have changed, and so today, students in

Libya can again learn the English language in some of the local schools set up by the British and other foreign nations.

THE CURRICULUM OF PUBLIC SCHOOLS

General education in the MENA region consists of kindergarten (three- to five-year-olds), six years of primary school (grades 1–6), and three years each of intermediate/preparatory school (grades 7–9) and high or secondary school (grades 10–12). The core curriculum of all public schools is based upon what curriculum planners in the region deem to be essential knowledge that all schools should teach. In many of the countries, such as Saudi Arabia, Syria, Kuwait, Libya, and Bahrain, these include language arts and religious education. Curriculum design and implementation is the work of the Ministry of Education in each country. Members are drawn from the government and the general public, including special interest groups. The broad nature of the membership implies that the interests of all groups in the community will be served. This is one key element of the importance of focusing curriculum on local needs, values, and interests (Oliva, 2005).

PROGRAM OF STUDIES

On the attainment of independence when the management of education became the responsibility of local educators, the curriculum for all public schools underwent dramatic changes. These changes were made to help teachers provide children with the kind of education that will make them productive members of society. Although religion continues to play a major role in the curriculum of all public schools in the region, other courses are also given prominent attention. In most of the MENA countries, Arabic is the medium of instruction in all public schools.

A brief outline of the curriculum for public schools in Dubai, United Arab Emirates, includes:

- *Arabic Language:* Produced and distributed by the Ministry of Education, Arabic language is a course of twelve-plus-basic levels that is compulsory, for Arab students only, in grades K–12. The course is taught in Arabic in regular classrooms, with special classes in English for Arabs who are nonnative speakers.
- *English Language:* A compulsory course for all students from kindergarten through grade 12. The course includes reading and language arts subcourses that are presented at different levels and grades.
- *English Literature:* A five-level course that is given for all students in grades 7–11. The course includes a variety of literary works and pieces from modern, medieval, and ancient ages.
- *Science:* A compulsory twelve-level course, with the English language as a medium of instruction, in labs and regular classrooms. The science course at Dubai Modern

Education School (DMES) includes subcourses that are introduced at intermediate and advanced levels such as physics, biology, and chemistry.

- *Mathematics:* A compulsory twelve-level course, with the English language as a medium of instruction. Mathematics is given to all grades from 1 to 12, with geometry and calculus introduced at the high school level.
- *Information Technology:* A compulsory twelve-plus-basic-level course given in grades 1–12. The course goes through interval review processes and is subject to change every year to keep pace with the nonstop development of digital technology.
- *Geography:* A compulsory three-level course given to all students in grades 7–9. The Arabic language is the medium of instruction in this course; for those whose mother tongue is other than Arabic, the school assigns special classes and translated textbooks.
- *Social Studies:* A compulsory three-level course taught to all students in grades 4–6. Arabic is the medium of instruction in this course, and for non-Arabic speakers, the school assigns special classes and translated textbooks.

THE CORE CURRICULUM

The core curriculum in the Middle East and North Africa differs from country to country. The main goal of defining a core curriculum is to find common courses that all students will need before graduating from school. Oliva (2005, p. 256) has identified the main characteristics of the core curriculum:

- They constitute a portion of the curriculum that is required for all students.
- They integrate, unify, or fuse subject matter.
- Their content centers on problems that cut across the disciplines.
- The primary method of learning is problem solving, using all applicable subject matter.
- They are organized into blocks of time, usually two to three periods under a "core" teacher (with possible use of additional teachers and others as resource persons).
- They encourage teachers to plan with students.
- They provide pupil guidance.

Among the Arab states, the core curriculum includes the following:

- Language arts, such as Arabic, French, or English
- Mathematics
- Sciences
- Computer education
- Religious education
- Islamic education
- Mathematics
- National/Social studies, including geography and history

Table 3.1 shows a typical school curriculum for grades 1–12 in the United Arab Emirates. This was the curriculum used for the 2006/2007 school year.

Table 3.1
Ministry of Education Curriculum Subjects for the Academic Year 2006/2007 in Dubai, United Arab Emirates

Grades 1–3	Grades 4–6	Grades 7–9	Grades 10–12
Islamic Education	Islamic Education	Islamic Education	Islamic Education
Arabic Language	Arabic Language	Arabic Language	Arabic Language
English Language	English Language	English Language	English Language
Mathematics	Social Studies	History	History
Sciences	Mathematics	Geography	Geography
Computer	Sciences	National Studies	Mathematics
Physical Education	Computer	Mathematics	Chemistry
Arts	Physical Education	Sciences	Biology
	Arts	Computer	Physics
		Physical Education	Geology
		Arts	Computer
			Physical Education

Source: Compiled from UNESCO International Bureau of Education, 6th Edition, 2008: http://www.ibe.unesco.org/countries/WDE/2006/index.html.

THE SCHOOL TIMETABLE

The weekly school timetable is based upon the general curriculum standards drawn up by the national governments. The number of weekly hours for each course depends upon the emphasis placed on particular subjects. In general, core curriculum courses are taught more often than courses that are not deemed to be part of the core. In Syria, in the primary school curriculum, the Arabic language forms the core of the curriculum (see tables 3.2–3.4).

CURRICULUM TRACKS

In the Middle East and North Africa, curricula for secondary schools are divided into tracks. This is done to ensure that the educational system meets the needs of the diverse students in the region. Designing the curriculum to meet the talents, needs, and aspirations of the individual is a hallmark of educational excellence because of individual differences. Human beings differ in their talents and learning styles, and therefore, for learning to be effective, the program must be structured to meet the needs of individuals (Oliva, 2005).

In Bahrain, the curriculum is divided into the scientific, commercial, literary, and technical tracks. Students in the scientific track are required to take sixty-two credit hours of courses in science, including mathematics, physics, chemistry, biology, and geology. They are also required to earn an extra twelve credit hours in their field of specialization (see table 3.5).

Students in the literary track take compulsory core courses in the social sciences. These courses include the Arabic and English languages, Islamic

Table 3.2
Weekly Lesson Timetable, Primary School, Syria, 2002

Subject	Number of weekly periods in each grade					
	I	II	III	IV	V	VI
Religious education	2	2	3	3	3	3
Arabic language	11	11	10	10	8	8
Foreign language	—	—	—	—	3	3
Mathematics	5	5	5	5	5	5
Social studies	1	1	1	2	4	4
Science and health education	2	2	3	3	3	3
Music education	2	2	2	2	1	1
Physical education	3	3	3	3	2	2
Art education	2	2	3	2	1	1
Subtotal	28	28	30	30	30	30
Vanguard activities	2	2	2	2	2	2
Educational activities	2	2	—	—	—	—
Total weekly periods	*32*	*32*	*32*	*32*	*32*	*32*

Source: International Bureau of Education, http://www.ibe.unesco.org/countries/country Dossier/timestables/TSyrianAR.pdf.

education, history, geography, economics, sociology, philosophy, and psychology. They are also required to take extra credit hours in their field of specialization (see table 3.6).

In the commercial track, students study to become financial advisors, bankers, and accountants. They therefore take courses that are related to their field. These include accounting, mathematics, commerce, typing, economics, information technology, and insurance (see table 3.7).

Apart from these courses, for their specialized elective courses, students take six credit hours in financial accounting, banking, insurance, travel agencies, marketing, mathematics, sales, secretarial practice, or electronic typewriting.

Students who opt for the technical track prepare for careers in industry, education, and business. They take courses in mathematics, mechanics, science, industry, and drawing (see table 3.8).

CURRICULUM REFORM

Curriculum reform has taken place in all the countries in the Middle East and North Africa since the beginning of the twentieth century. These reforms are meant "to stress local, environmental and national studies to reduce the attention paid to ... studies of the history and geography of other parts of the world" (Qubain, 1966, p. 79). These reforms are also designed to offer students the opportunity to learn relevant and valuable skills that will make them

Table 3.3
Weekly Lesson Timetable, Preparatory Education (Lower Secondary), Syria, 2002

Subject	Number of weekly periods in each grade		
	I	II	III
Religious education	2	2	2
Arabic language (including handwriting)	6	6	6
Foreign language	5	5	5
Mathematics	4	4	5
Social studies (history, geography, and national socialist education)	4	4	4
General science	3	4	4
Drawing	1	1	1
Practical subjects (manual works)	2	2	1
Music and anthems	1	2	—
Agriculture (boys) or needlework and home economics (girls)	2	2	2
Military training	2	2	2
Total weekly periods	*32*	*34*	*32*
Physical education (boys)	2	2	2
Physical education (girls)	2	2	1

Source: International Bureau of Education, http://www.ibe.unesco.org/countries/country Dossier/timestables/TSyrianAR.pdf.

competitive in national and international arenas. These reforms have brought about significant changes in education for all students in the region, especially girls.

Although the education of girls in the region has a long history, it has always been subordinated to the education of boys. Even when girls were encouraged by parents and the government to go to school, in many instances, they were not permitted to engage in all aspects of the curriculum. One area was physical education. Today, as a result of the changes that have taken place in the organization of schools, girls are encouraged to take physical education, although a few people in the region still do not favor it. In Qatar, physical education forms part of the education of girls. Girls in the lower secondary schools take the same number of physical education classes as boys.

In Libya, the following are some of the major changes that have taken place in the curriculum of all public schools:

- Changes have taken place in science and mathematics education.
- Educational technology has been added to the school curriculum.

Table 3.4
Weekly Lesson Timetable, General Secondary Education, Syria, 2002

Subject	Number of weekly periods in each grade				
	I	II		III	
		Sci*	Lit	Sci	Lit
Religious education	2	2	2	2	2
Arabic language	6	4	7	4	8
Foreign language	5	5	8	5	7
Principles of philosophy and sociology	1	—	—	—	—
Logic and humanities	—	2	—	—	—
Arab society, principles of economics, and general philosophy	—	—	3	—	—
Philosophy	—	—	—	—	5
History	2	1	3	—	3
Geography	2	—	3	—	3
Mathematics	4	6	—	8	—
Computer science	2	2	—	—	—
Statistics and science	—	—	2	—	—
Physics	2	4	—	5	—
Chemistry	2	2	—	2	—
Biology	2	3	—	3	—
Art education	1	—	1	—	—
Physical education	1	1	1	—	1
National socialist education	1	1	1	1	1
Military training	2	2	2	2	2
Total weekly periods	35	35	33	32	32

* Sci = Science; Lit = Literary

Source: International Bureau of Education, http://www.ibe.unesco.org/countries/country Dossier/timestables/TSyrianAR.pdf.

- The content of some social science subjects such as Arabic language, history, and geography has been expanded.
- The English language has been included in the school curriculum, starting from the fifth grade.
- The science curriculum has been expanded to include environmental education.
- Human rights education has been added to Islamic education.

TECHNICAL AND VOCATIONAL EDUCATION

Technical and vocational training has left an indelible mark on the education of students in the Middle East and North Africa (World Bank, 2005). Interest in technical and vocational education has been quite stable among students in the region. In 1999, nearly three million students were enrolled in the

Table 3.5
Scientific Track for Secondary Education in Bahrain

Compulsory Courses for All Science Majors		
Field	Credit Hours	No. of Periods
Mathematics	18	270
Physics	18	270
Chemistry	12	180
Biology	12	180
Geology	2	30
Total	*62*	*930*

Elective Specialized Courses: *Students Are Required to Choose 12 Credit Hours from This Section*	
No. of Courses	Credit Hours
Three Courses in Mathematics	10
Three Courses in Physics	10
Three Courses in Chemistry	8
Three Courses in Biology	10
Three Courses in Geology	6

Source: Ministry of Education, Bahrain, 2007. http://www.education.goc.bh/english/schools/index.asp.

numerous technical and vocational institutions in the region. The number slightly increased in the 2004 academic year.

In the Middle East and North Africa, technical and vocational educational programs are designed by governments to offer students the opportunity to acquire a skill that will allow them to enter the job market after graduation (Calvert & Al-Shetaiwi, 2002). Technical and vocational education form part of secondary education. Students who do not wish to enter college or university enroll in these institutions to acquire skills that are in high demand in the region (Cook, 2000). It is also an attempt on the part of educational planners to help make graduating students productive members of society (Mott, 1965).

In Kuwait, the real development of technical and vocational education started in 1975 following a recommendation from UNESCO. Among other things, UNESCO recommended that "technical-vocational education in Kuwait develop structures within various occupations and elevate the standard of labor force in the country" (Verma, 1981, p. 54). Following the UNESCO recommendations in 1978, the Kuwaiti government opened a secondary vocational school for boys. This school offered "academic and vocational courses. All students take general academic courses in the beginning and later select a

Table 3.6
Literary Track for Secondary Education in Bahrain

Compulsory Specialized Courses		
Field	Credit Hours	No. of Periods
Arabic Language	14	180
English Language	12	180
Islamic Education	4	60
History	10	150
Geography	10	150
Economics	4	60
Sociology	2	30
Philosophy	2	30
Psychology	2	30
Total	*62*	*930*

Elective Specialized Courses: *Students Are Required to Choose 12 Credit Hours from This Section*	
No. of Courses	Credit Hours
Three Courses in Arabic Language	10
Three Courses in English Language	10
Three Courses in French Language	10
Four Courses in Islamic Law	8
Two Courses in Social Studies	4
Two Courses in Philosophy and Logic	4

Source: Ministry of Education, Bahrain, 2007. http://www.education.goc.bh/english/schools/index.asp.

course of studies in the arts, sciences, commerce, or industry according to their interests and abilities" (Verma, 1981, pp. 55–56). Two years later, the government established a separate secondary vocational school for girls. As Verma (1981) has indicated:

Kuwait is tackling the problem of technical-vocational education with energy and resourcefulness. Its internal expansion of primary, secondary, and university training has been supplemented by generous grants to citizens to study abroad and by generous aid to other developing companies, where several technical-vocational institutions have been paid for and handsomely endowed. Kuwait sees its long term development within the context of the developing world as a whole, rather than as an isolated pocket of wealth with good intention. (p. 57)

Another country in the MENA region that has made progress in the development of secondary vocational education is Libya. These secondary schools

Table 3.7
Commercial Track for Secondary Education in Bahrain

Compulsory Specialized Courses		
Field	Credit Hours	No. of Periods
Accounting (Arabic and English)	10	150
Banking	4	60
Financial Math	8	120
Basis of Commerce	4	60
Economics	4	60
Insurance	2	30
Office Practice (Arabic and English)	10	150
Information Technology	8	120
Arabic Typing	4	60
English Typing	4	60
Trade and Labor	4	60
Total	*62*	*930*

Source: Ministry of Education, Bahrain, 2007. http://www.education.goc.bh/english/schools/index.asp.

Table 3.8
Technical Track for Secondary Education in Bahrain

Supported Courses for Specialization				
	Technical		Applied	
Field	Credit Hours	Periods	Credit Hours	Periods
Science	16	240	8	120
Mathematics	18	270	12	180
Mechanics	6	90	4	60
Total	*40*	*600*	*24*	*360*

Supported Courses				
	Technical		Applied	
Field	Credit Hours	Periods	Credit Hours	Periods
Industrial Principles	22	330	18	270
Technical Drawing	14	210	14	210
Practical Studies	84	1260	104	1560
Total	*120*	*1800*	*136*	*2040*

Source: Ministry of Education, Bahrain, 2007. http://www.education.goc.bh/english/schools/index.asp.

include five main specialty areas (Libyan National Commission for Education, Culture, and Science, 2004):

1. Mechanical vocations, including ten specializations:

    - General mechanics
    - Welding and steel iron works
    - Elevator technology
    - Foundry
    - Car mechanics
    - Agricultural machine mechanics
    - Carpentry and furniture upholstery
    - Heavy vehicle mechanics
    - Manufacturing tools and equipment
    - Air-conditioning maintenance

2. Electrical vocations, including nine specializations:

    - Computer technologies
    - Industrial electrical extensions
    - Transformation and distribution of electricity power
    - Computer software
    - Operation control and measuring devices
    - House electrical extensions
    - Television and radio devices
    - Telephone and telecommunication devices
    - Electrical tools maintenance

3. Engineering vocations, including seven specializations:

    - Building, bricks, and concrete
    - Paving and tile-laying
    - Concrete carpentry
    - Coating and decoration
    - Plumbing and sanitation
    - Architectural design
    - Land survey

4. Hospitality vocations, including four specializations:

    - Hotel management
    - Food production
    - Frontal circles
    - Serving arts

5. Fishery vocations, including two specializations:

    - Fishing
    - Boat building

The main goal of the Libyan government in developing these institutions is to enable all students in the country to acquire valuable but simple skills to gainfully participate in the labor market.

Despite the efforts and reforms the governments in the region have made in the provision of vocational and technical education, these programs are not very popular among students in the Middle East and North Africa for several reasons. The World Bank (2005) sums up the reasons as follows:

- Large numbers of those who are able to continue from basic to secondary education are tracked into poorer quality vocational streams.
- Vocational streams are not conceived as quality education, and graduates have limited opportunities to access post-secondary education.
- Technical and Vocational Education and Training (TVET), as an alternative to general education, has resulted in poor quality programmes. This affects its acceptance among students and parents.
- Students from lower socio-economic backgrounds are over-represented in vocational education streams, thus raising equity concerns.
- There is no evidence that restricting access to general education at the secondary and higher levels improves the quality of education.
- Employment trends in the region point to an increasing mismatch between education outcomes and skills needs, especially from vocational institutions. (p. 19)

TEXTBOOKS

Nearly all the countries have reformed the textbooks used in schools to conform to the changes made in the curriculum. These textbooks have been reworked to reflect local history, culture, and geography. In Libya, to ensure that the content of textbooks conforms to the new curriculum, the government set up a committee that worked with UNESCO to review the textbooks to be used in all public schools.

Apart from revisions made to the textbook content, most of the countries publish their textbooks locally and distribute them free of charge. Turkey during the 2003/2004 academic year distributed more than eighty-one million books to public primary schools in the country (Turkey, 2004). The free textbooks have made schooling available and affordable for millions of children, especially those from poor and rural areas.

In many of the countries in the Middle East and North Africa such as Algeria, Tunisia, Egypt, Lebanon, and Jordan, the image of girls and women has changed in textbooks. Instead of the traditional role of a woman as a mother and wife, she is seen in modern social studies textbooks as a scientist, doctor, teacher, or public official. Textbooks are revised periodically to reflect changing circumstances and societal needs.

EDUCATIONAL TECHNOLOGY

One of the major innovations in the curriculum is the introduction of educational technology. In all the MENA countries, educational technology has become an integral part of teaching and learning activities. To make the integration of technology into teaching and learning easier and more seamless, teachers are given training in the use of common technology tools either at home or abroad (Monk, Swain, Ghrist, & Riddle, 2003). Many of the universities have set up education departments that have included educational technology as components of its course structure. Riyadh University in Saudi Arabia and the University of Jordan were some of the institutions in the region that first provided training in educational technology for teachers locally (Al-Abed, 1986). Countries such as the United Kingdom, the United States, France, Germany, Japan, and Australia often provide funds and training facilities for teachers in the region.

As a result of the training teachers in the region have received, they are able to use educational technology to deliver instruction in several ways. These include the following activities listed by Gagné, Wager, Golas, and Keller (2005)

- Online course materials and syllabus (document sharing)
- Online or computer-based software, courseware, or tutorials
- Group activities (in person or online)
- Peer tutoring, collaboration
- Email or voice-mail discussions
- Journal writing (reflective learning)
- Calendar of events, course announcements, and bulletin boards
- Chart-room discussions, threaded discussions, or guided discussions
- Video-conferencing, audio conferencing
- Web searches (critical evaluation)
- Exploration activities or discovery learning
- Online graphics, video, and voice clips
- Online interactive quizzes and other assessments. (p. 225)

Students have to follow rules and regulations as they use technology, especially when they go on the World Wide Web. The rules are designed to ensure the safety of the students as they get on the Internet. Below is the computer acceptable use policy for British International School in Riyadh, Saudi Arabia (British International School, 2006).

Responsible Internet Use
Rules for Pupils, Years 1–5

These rules help us to be fair to others and keep everyone safe.

- I will ask permission before using the Internet.
- I will use only my own network login.
- I will only look at or delete my own files.
- I understand that I must not bring software or disks into school without permission.
- I will only e-mail people I know, or my teacher has approved.
- The messages I send will be polite and sensible.
- I understand that I must never give my home address or phone number, or arrange to meet someone.

- I will ask for permission before opening an e-mail or an e-mail attachment sent by someone I do not know.
- I will not use Internet chat.
- If I see anything I am unhappy with or I receive messages I do not like, I will tell a teacher immediately.
- I understand that the school may check my computer files and the Internet sites I visit.
- I understand that if I deliberately break these rules, I may not be allowed to use the Internet or computers.

Responsible Internet Use
Rules for Pupils, Years 6–11

The computer system is owned by the school. This responsible Internet Use Statement helps to protect students, staff, and the school by clearly stating what use of the computer resources is acceptable and what is not.

- Irresponsible use may result in the loss of Internet access.
- Network access must be made via the user's authorized account and password, which must not be given to any other person.
- School computer and Internet use must be appropriate to the student's education.
- Copyright and intellectual property rights must be respected.
- E-mail should be written carefully and politely, particularly as messages may be forwarded or printed and be seen by unexpected readers.
- Users are responsible for e-mail they send and for contacts made.
- Anonymous messages and chain letters are not permitted.
- The use of chat rooms is not allowed.
- The school Information and Communication Technology (ICT) systems may not be used for private purposes, unless the Principal has given permission for that use.
- Use for personal financial gain, gambling, political purposes or advertising is not permitted.
- ICT system security must be respected; it is a criminal offence to use a computer for a purpose not permitted by the system owner.

British International School, Riyadh
Rules for Pupils, Foundation 1 & 2

These rules help us to stay safe on the Internet. Think, then click.

- We only use the Internet when an adult is with us.
- We can click on the buttons or links when we know what they do.
- We can search the Internet with an adult.
- We always ask if we get lost on the Internet.
- We can send and open emails together.
- We can write polite and friendly emails to people that we know.

THE CURRICULUM OF PRIVATE AND FOREIGN SCHOOLS

In the private schools set up by missionaries or expatriates, the curriculum has different features. Although the Quran may not be the basis for the curriculum's design and implementation, students and teachers do not have the freedom to teach courses or programs that are contrary to what the Quran teaches. In other words, the curriculum of all private educational institutions is subject to approval by the curriculum planning committee in each country. This is meant to ensure that the quality of education the students get from the private schools is in alignment with the values and standards prescribed by each government.

The curriculum of each foreign-based school follows the curriculum of the parent country. For instance, all the British schools in the MENA region follow the curriculum designed for the schools in Great Britain. The United Kingdom has more than sixty-six private schools in the region, and all of them follow the British curriculum. These schools serve students from different countries in the region. In some respects, however, the British schools follow the tradition of the host country. For instance, in Great Britain, the school week starts Monday and ends Friday, but in the Middle East and North Africa, the school week begins Sunday and ends Thursday.

Language Requirements

Children who enroll in a school set up by a foreign country must learn to speak the language of that country. For example, children who study in a school set up by the British must learn to speak and write English. In the same way, children who enroll in a school established by the French must learn to speak and write French. Although Arabic is taught in all schools, it does not form part of the core curriculum in privately funded educational institutions. In some cases, it serves as an elective course.

Extracurricular Activities

In addition to classroom instruction, students participate in extracurricular activities such as drama, soccer, rounders, netball, swimming, basketball, volleyball, tennis, and track and field activities. In some of the schools, students form clubs and engage in activities such as interschool debate or sports contests. The variety of activities gives all students the opportunity to engage in games that are of interest to them.

SUMMARY

The curricula for schools in the Middle East and North Africa have been redesigned to reflect the interests, values, and aspirations of students in the region. The influence of foreign content on the schools has been greatly curtailed. Now, local languages such as Arabic are the main language of instruction in all public schools. Private schools do not have to use Arabic as the language of instruction, but they must include Arabic in their curriculum. Foreign countries in the region that still influence curriculum development include France, Great Britain, and the United States.

REFERENCES

Al-Abed, A. B. (1986). Educational technology in the Arab World. *International Review of Education, 32*(3), 350–53.

British International School. (2006). *British International School: Internet policy.* Riyadh, Saudi Arabia: Author.

Calvert, J. R., & Al-Shetaiwi, A. S. (2002). Exploring the mismatch between skills and jobs for women in Saudi Arabia in technical and vocational areas: The view of Saudi Arabian private sector business managers. *International Journal of Training and Development, 6*(2), 112–24.

Cook, B. J. (2000). Egypt's national education debate. *Comparative Education, 36*(4), 477–90.

Gagné, R. M., Wager, W. W., Golas, K. C., & Keller, J. M. (2005). *Principles of instructional design.* Belmont, CA: Wadsworth.

Libyan National Commission for Development of Education, Culture, and Science. (2004). *The development of education in the great Jamahiriya.* A National report presented to the International Conference on Education, Session 47, 8–11 September, Geneva. Available at http://www.ibe.unesco.org/International/ICE47/English/Natreps/reports/libya_en.pdf.

Monk, M., Swain, J., Ghrist, M., & Riddle, W. (2003). Notes on classroom practice and ownership and use of personal computers amongst Egyptian science and mathematics teachers. *Education and Information Technologies, 8*(1), 83–95.

Mott, P. E. (1965). *The organization of society.* Englewood Cliffs, NJ: Prentice-Hall.

Oliva, P. F. (2005). *Developing the curriculum.* Boston: Pearson.

Qubain, F. I. (1966). *Education and science in the Arab world.* Baltimore: Johns Hopkins University Press.

Turkey. Ministry of National Education. (2004). *The Turkish education system and development in education, 2004.* Report presented to 47th session of the International Conference on Education, Geneva, September 8–11. Available at http://www.ibe.unesco.org/International/ICE47/English/Natreps/reports/turkey.pdf.

Verma, D. (1981). Kuwait's system of technical-vocational education: An investment in future. *Community College Review, 9*(2), 53–57.

World Bank. (2005). *Reforming technical vocational education and training in the Middle East and North Africa: Experiences and challenges.* Luxembourg: European Training Foundations.

Chapter 4

THE EDUCATION SYSTEMS IN THE MIDDLE EAST AND NORTH AFRICA

The education system in the Middle East and North Africa is under the control of the central government in each country. In this region, each government views education as a key to national development (Akkari, 2004). During the colonial period, education here was essentially under the control of foreign educators. Primary, secondary, and higher education opportunities were few and were mostly controlled and managed by foreign missionaries and other educators. The medium of instruction was the language of the European colonial power, usually English or French. Arabic, the language of most of the people in the region, played little of no significant role in the education of the vast majority of the students.

In many of the Middle East and North Africa (MENA) countries such as Algeria, Tunisia, Egypt, Syria, and Iraq, kuttabs and madrasahs were the other avenue that provided literacy skills to hundreds of children. The kuttabs and madrasahs existed side by side with the foreign and the few public schools to provide education for children. They basically provided religious education to the students, although the curriculum also included a few secular subjects such as mathematics, astronomy, geometry, and Arabic literature. The medium of instruction was Arabic. The students did not have to pay fees to join the madrasahs, which served as boarding institutions for the students. The students were supervised daily by their instructors.

The curriculum content of the kuttabs and madrasahs later proved to be inadequate to meet the needs of the students in a changing society, however. Contact with the Western world brought about changes in all the societies in the Middle East and North Africa. Writing, reading, and computing skills became the standard for determining the status of the job a person held. Secular educational institutions therefore came to overshadow the kuttabs and madrasahs in popularity (Nasser, 2004).

With this as the backdrop, upon the attainment of independence, each country embarked upon a national project to review, revise, and expand education to reflect local interests and aspirations. In this process, each government diversified the school curriculum to reflect national pride and made Arabic the official language to be used in all public schools. The MENA countries all invested huge national resources to redesign the educational system, and the school curriculum was greatly affected. The number of hours devoted to religious studies was reduced everywhere. Science and mathematics courses were also redesigned to embrace technical and scientific developments, and new subjects such as educational technology were added to the programs of studies for students at various levels. Social sciences and humanities were also developed, with special emphasis on Arabic-language and Islamic education. The new educational system was divided into several sectors: pre-primary, primary, preparatory, lower secondary, secondary, vocational, and higher education.

PRIVATE SCHOOLS

Numerous private education institutions are found in the MENA region. There are two main categories of private educational institutions in the region: private international schools and local private schools. Local private schools are often subjected to national educational policies. International private schools, on the other hand, get permission from local governments to modify their curricula to reflect international educational programs. Because of this, most international private educational institutions provide coeducation, although they are free to operate single-sex schools.

Private schools range from primary to university level. Each country has set up guidelines for the establishment and administration of private education. All proprietors of private schools must seek approval for their programs from the central government. Issues like fees, holidays, and curriculum content are all discussed with the ministry of education in each country.

THE SCHOOL YEAR

The school year varies from country to country. In Turkey, it consists of 180 working days. The academic year begins in mid-September and ends by the middle of June. In the United Arab Emirates, the school year consists of about 150 days. This is defined each year by the Ministry of Education to avoid conflict with national activities and holidays. In Libya, the school year lasts about 200 days for pre-primary and primary education and about 230 days at the secondary level. At the tertiary level, the school year is thirty-five weeks long.

DURATION OF PRIMARY EDUCATION

Primary education is compulsory in the region. Its duration is five or six years for all students. There are five years of primary education in Kuwait and six in Algeria. Children start primary school at the age of 5 or 6 and most students move to the next stage, middle school, at the age of 11 or 12. Altogether, compulsory education lasts nine or ten years in many of the countries.

CLASS SIZE

Class sizes in the primary and secondary schools vary from country to country and between urban and rural schools. In many of the countries in the Middle East and North Africa, class sizes may range from twenty-two to as many as fifty students. In the private schools, there are usually twenty to thirty-five students per class. In Libya, the average class size is about thirty. However, in regions with high population density, average class size can be as high as sixty pupils. In the public elementary schools, average class size may be as high as forty pupils in Egypt and as low as twenty-eight pupils in Israel, Jordan, and Tunisia (UNESCO, International Bureau of Education, 2004).

DOUBLE-SHIFT SCHOOLS

Double-shift schools exist in some of the urban school districts to provide schooling opportunities for students in regions with higher population concentrations (Herrera, 2003). Double-shift schools are common in Egypt and Turkey. However, it is the aim of all governments in the region to eliminate double-shift schools because of the problem of organization and administration.

SCHOOL UNIFORMS AT PUBLIC, RELIGIOUS, AND PRIVATE SCHOOLS

Students going to school in the Middle East and North Africa are often requested by school authorities to wear school uniforms at the primary and high school levels. In both public and private educational institutions, students are required to wear school uniforms. In Saudi Arabia, boys in public schools are required by law to wear traditional clothes for class, including the *thobe* and *shumaq*. Teenage girls in public schools wear traditional *abayas* over white, long-sleeve shirts and long skirts to and from school. They wear scarves (*hijab*) to cover the hair.

In private international schools, students wear Western-style uniforms rather than traditional clothing. Boys and girls wear different uniforms to school. The boys usually wear short- or long-sleeve shirts over shorts or trousers. Girls typically wear short- or long-sleeve shirts over skirts. Students are sometimes required to wear shoes or sandals. In some countries, boys and girls in international private schools are expected to wear neckties to school.

No uniforms are required for pre-primary children, although some schools encourage their pupils to wear uniforms. However, in the private schools, they are urged to take prescribed uniforms to school for physical education class. For example, the physical education (PE) requirements for the British

International School of Al Khobar in the United Arab Emirates are clearly stated in the school handbook for students:

All students take part in the school's physical education programme. Each element of PE requires the proper school PE kit, which comprises house T-shirts (available from the school shop) and white shorts (available in town), as well as swimming trunks (mid-thigh length and not Bermuda shorts/baggy shorts which impede the swimmers) or costumes. White socks with plain black or white gym shoes or trainers are the required footwear. A labelled towel is also required.

Fashion trainers and plimsolls are unsuitable for PE activities and are not allowed. Properly designed athletics/running shoes ie cross-training shoes are required. Please feel free to contact the PE coordinator for advice if required.

All students come to school wearing their PE kit. Attention is paid to due decorum, especially in the case of our older students, who should be appropriately covered when they travel to school. All students wear their normal school uniform home on PE days. (British International School of Al Khobar, 2006, pp. 26–27)

PRE-PRIMARY EDUCATION

Pre-primary school begins at the age of 3 and ends at 5. The aim of pre-primary education is to prepare young children to learn how to learn and also how to develop positive relations with other students before they enter primary school. As described by the Sultanate of Oman, the purposes for setting up pre-primary schools are:

- Promoting a balanced intellectual, spiritual, emotional, social and moral development of the child's personality;
- Strengthening the Islamic principles, consolidating the Arabic language and developing the children's sentiments towards their country and its various symbols and traditions;
- Teaching the child to adopt positive attitudes and behavior and enhancing the spirit of co-operation among children;
- Developing the child's attitude towards the arts;
- Acquainting the children with certain aspects, activities and social events characteristic of the Sultanate of Oman, and giving them the opportunity to participate therein;
- Giving the child the opportunity to exercise intellectual and social processes and skills that are supposed to be developed through the kindergarten curriculum, such as the ability to classify, compare and establish chronology;
- Giving the children the opportunity to exercise the maximum amount of activity and allowing them to express their sentiments, ideas and questions;
- Preparing children for school education. (UNESCO, 2006b, p. 5)

The teaching methods are usually in the form of play. Such teaching methods are proven to be effective in helping young children master new concepts and skills necessary for learning when they enter primary school.

Teachers endeavor to make the classroom atmosphere as comfortable and as friendly as possible. They try to play the role of parents at this level of education. Memorization is not often the case here. Young children are still developing new concepts, and they have a hard time understanding abstract ideas because their brains at this stage are not well developed enough to master abstract ideas. Subjects taught at this level include fundamentals of mathematics, reading and social studies, Arabic, English, art, music, Islamic studies, and physical education. The implementation of these subjects varies between public and private schools. For instance, in the public pre-primary schools, English is not taught. However, in the private schools organized by the British or Americans, young children are taught English.

In Israel, subjects taught in preschools include the following:

- Linguistic skills and general literacy (spoken and written language, symbolic language, the language of mathematics, artistic expression);
- Learning skills (cognitive skills, inquiry and problem-solving at developmentally appropriate levels of complexity);
- Social-emotional skills: self-awareness and assertiveness, cooperation and peer relationship, solving social conflicts, rules of discourse, recognizing and accepting differences between people (mutual respect, aid, and tolerance), recognizing the importance and significance of laws and social rules, familiarity with different cultures, maintaining personal hygiene and health, protecting the environment, safety and security, cultural consumption and the media;
- Physical-movement skills (daily experience with movement and the use of outdoor play equipment, physical training and ball games); and
- Educational contents for formulating a common cultural-social-civil foundation. (UNESCO, 2006a, p. 11)

Children in pre-primary schools in Bahrain follow similar curricular activities. The curriculum for pre-primary children in the Bahrain Bayan School, an independent, nonprofit school in Isa Town, Bahrain, consists of the following:

- *Personal Social Development* focuses on children learning how to work, play, co-operate with others, and function in a group beyond the family. It covers important aspects of personal, social, and academic development, including personal values and an understanding of self and of others.
- *Language and Literacy* covers language development and provides the foundation for literacy. Children are helped to acquire competence in English and Arabic as soon as possible, making use, where appropriate, of their developing understanding and skills in the other language. The focus is on children's developing competence in talking and listening and in becoming readers and writers.
- *Mathematics and Problem Solving* covers mathematical understanding and provides the foundation for numeracy. The focus is on achievement through practical activities and on understanding and using language in the development of simple mathematical ideas.
- *Physical Development* focuses on children's developing physical control, mobility, awareness of space and manipulative skills in indoor and outdoor environments. It includes establishing positive attitudes towards a healthy and active way of life.
- *Creative Development* focuses on the development of children's imagination and their ability to communicate and to express ideas and feelings in creative ways.

- *Knowledge and Understanding of the World* focuses on children's developing knowledge and understanding of their environment, other people and features of the world. This provides a foundation for historical, geographical, scientific and technological learning. (Bahrain Bayan School, 2005)

Although pre-primary education is not compulsory in the MENA region, available figures indicate that many parents encourage their children to participate in it.

PRIMARY EDUCATION

In the MENA countries, primary education is free and compulsory for all students. Each country in the region has its own objectives, laws, and policies governing primary education. In words similar to those used throughout the region, Jordan has summed up the main objectives for promoting primary education as preparing students to:

- Follow social behavior rules and take into account commendable social traditions, habits, and values;
- Absorb basic scientific facts and generalizations and their experimental bases, and use them to explain natural phenomena;
- Think scientifically, using the process of observation, data collection, organization, analysis, deduction and making decisions and judgments based on them;
- Comprehend the scientific basis of the forms of technology and use them properly;
- Be able to perform handicraft skills matching their abilities and interests, make an effort to develop them, and have respect for manual work owing to its basic function in social life;
- Be aware of the importance of their physical fitness and health, and practice suitable sport and health activities;
- Be keen on the safety, cleanliness, beauty, and wealth of their environment;
- Express their talents, special abilities, and creative aspects;
- Accept themselves, respect others, consider their feelings, and appreciate their merits and achievements;
- Assimilate diligence, work, persistence and self-dependence values in achievement, realization of self-capability, earning a living and self-sufficiency. (UNESCO, International Bureau of Education, 2006; World Data on Education, 6th Edition)

Each country in the region has formulated its own school laws and policies. In the United Arab Emirates, Federal Law No. 11 (1972), which deals with compulsory education, states that

education is compulsory in the primary stage and free at all stages for U.A.E. nationals; that it is the duty of the state to provide school buildings, textbooks and teachers; that compulsory education starts at the primary stage at age 6 and lasts as specified by regulations and laws; and that the Ministry lays down the curricula, scheme of work, subjects to be taught, methods of promotion, number of school years and whatever else may be acquired for good performance. (UNESCO, International Bureau of Education, 2006, United Arab Emirates)

Israel introduced its Compulsory Education Law in 1949, one year after the country became independent. The law was reformed in 1968. The Compulsory Education Law states that

compulsory education applies to all children between the ages of 5 (compulsory kindergarten) and 15 (grade 10) inclusive. This education is provided free of charge. In addition, the law provides for free education for adolescents aged 16–17, as well as for 18-year-olds who did not complete their schooling in Grade XI in accordance with the curriculum. The state is responsible for provision of free primary education under this law. Maintenance of official educational institutions, however, is the joint responsibility of the State and the local education authority. Parents have the right to choose one of the recognized educational trends for their children.

Important additions to the original version of this law include a prohibition against discrimination on the grounds of ethnic origin, a prohibition against discrimination in acceptance, placement, and advancement of pupils as well as a prohibition against punishing pupils for actions or omissions on the part of their parents. (Israel, 1996, p. 2)

The compulsory age for education in the MENA countries starts at the age of 6 and ends between the ages of 14 and 17 in all public institutions. The duration for primary education is six years (see table 4.1).

PRIMARY SCHOOL ENROLLMENTS

Largely as a result of governmental involvement in the provision of education in the MENA region, enrollments in primary schools have been increasing over the years. Enrollments are consistently high in all the countries in the region. For instance, Lebanon in 2000 had a total primary school enrollment of nearly 500,000. The comparable figure for Morocco in the same year was nearly 4 million, and Syria recorded about 3.5 million students. These are healthy indications of the efforts of the governments in the region to make basic education affordable and open to all.

In many of the countries, students get certificates after completing primary education. In Turkey, Egypt, and Libya, students get a diploma after successfully completing primary school education.

SECONDARY SCHOOL ENROLLMENTS

All the countries in the Middle East and North Africa place emphasis on secondary education. This is because the quality of education the students receive at this level determines the academic programs of students who enter

Table 4.1
Compulsory Education in Middle East and North Africa

Countries	Compulsory Education Age Range	Primary Education	
		Entrance Age	Duration
Algeria	6–14	6	6
Bahrain	—	6	6
Egypt (p)*	6–13	6	5
Iraq	6–11	6	6
Israel (p)*	5–15	6	6
Jordan (p)*	6–15	6	6
Kuwait	6–13	6	4
Lebanon	6–15	6	6
Libya	6–14	6	6
Morocco	6–14	6	6
Oman	—	6	6
Palestinian Authority	6–15	6	4
Qatar	6–17	6	6
Saudi Arabia	6–11	6	6
Sudan	6–13	6	6
Syria	6–14	6	4
Tunisia (p)*	6–16	6	6
Turkey	6–14	6	6
United Arab Emirates	6–14	6	5
Yemen	6–14	6	6

Source: UNESCO Institute for Statistics (2007).
(p) = data for the reference year or more recent years are provisional.

college or university for further studies. The main objectives of general secondary education as outlined by the state of Bahrain are:

- preparing the student, physically, mentally, morally, socially and nationally to be a mature individual and a good citizen
- educating him/her in the arts and sciences in order to prepare him/her for higher education
- preparing the student for life in general by providing him/her with sound values and knowledge about scientific trends, and the ability to solve problems of contemporary life, so that, after receiving vocational training, he/she can become a productive member of society. (UNESCO, International Bureau of Education, 2006, Bahrain)

These objectives are similar to the objectives identified by other countries in the region.

Students complete three years of intermediate or preparatory education before being admitted to secondary school. The curriculum for the intermediate or preparatory stage includes studying Arabic, social studies, basic science, mathematics, and English; providing students with opportunities to acquire technical know-how and experience in practical matters of life; and developing students' capacity to think in order to develop their creativity (UNESCO, International Bureau of Education, 2006, Bahrain).

Recent innovations in the curricula of the intermediate level include:

- teaching Arabic language curricula in all third- and fourth-year classes
- developing English-language curricula
- introducing new subjects in the social studies curriculum such as the Iraqi invasion and the role of the United Nations, the Gulf Cooperation Council (GCC), the Islamic Conference Organization, and the League of Arab States in the liberation of Kuwait
- making use of educational technology

The secondary school programs are divided into two main sections: scientific and literary. The science sections include the teaching of mainly mathematics, physics, chemistry, and geology. The literary section includes history, geography, English, philosophy, and sociology.

Enrollments in secondary schools are showing significant improvement in all MENA countries. One interesting observation is that nearly all these countries see education as performing similar functions in the development of the region and therefore find it necessary to share ideas and information about school organization and administration. A case in point is that all the countries have now made school attendance compulsory for children under the age of 15 or 16. In some cases, especially in the Gulf States, the governments pay for textbooks, uniforms, and other tools that students may need to learn at school. Such bold ventures have motivated students to enroll in secondary schools.

GRADUATION REQUIREMENTS

Assessment of secondary students varies from country to country. However, the general trend is that students are assessed during various stages of the program. The grades students get at the end of their program determine their next stage in the education process.

DROPPING OUT OF SCHOOL

Dropping out of school is not the aim of most of the students attending school in Middle East and North Africa. In general, these students value education like any other students in the world. However, due to some unforeseen circumstances, a few students do drop out. Leaving school early was a common thing in the past, especially when educational facilities were very few.

The dropout rate was particularly high among girls, who at times went to school only to meet government regulations and not with any desire to acquire a certificate for landing a government or clerical job. Moreover, tradition was against girls attending school, and so whenever there was any financial crisis in the family, the girls had to drop out of school before the boys did (Qubain, 1966). Many girls also left school to enter into marriage, a ritual very much prized by parents. Akkari (2004) has identified factors that contribute in no small measure to the school dropout rates in the region, including:

A. the inadequate quantity and quality of elementary and secondary schools;
B. the excessively long distance from home to school, which is a particularly important obstacle for girls in rural areas;
C. the lack of parent responsiveness to the laws mandating compulsory schooling, in light of the low private economic returns of schooling;
D. the inability of schools to offer an attractive environment to children;
E. the economic difficulties of some families who are forced to put their children to work early. (p. 149)

Today, the school dropout rates have gone down considerably. Many parents have found the need to send all their children to school. Moreover, financial assistance provided by the governments and compulsory school attendance laws no longer make it easy for parent to keep their children out of school.

TEACHER EDUCATION

Courses in pedagogy are essential components of teacher education programs because, as Arends (2004) observes, "classroom management and instruction are highly related" (p. 178). El-Tawil (1984) also found out from a study in Egyptian schools that the effect of teacher qualification had a significant effect on the academic achievement of students. This, in effect, implies that teachers who receive training or are certified to teach can create a more healthy learning environment to promote student academic achievement.

To this end, all the countries in the Middle East and North Africa, through their ministry of education, have developed teacher education programs to train teachers who instruct in the region's schools. In many cases, teachers are required to hold a bachelor's degree and a teacher certification before they are permitted to teach.

Teacher education programs last four years. These programs are usually carried out in higher education institutions. For instance, the University of Bahrain has a well-developed teacher education program that offers enrollees the opportunity to earn a bachelor's degree and a certificate to teach various courses in the private and public schools. The College of Education at the University of Bahrain has several departments that offer training programs for teachers, including: Curriculum and Instruction, Educational Foundations and Administration, Educational Technology, Psychology, and Physical Education. The university prepares teachers for various degrees. The major ones are:

- Master of Education/Curriculum Development (M.Ed.)
- Diploma in Education, specialization in teaching
- Diploma in School Administration
- Diploma in Learning Resources and Information
- Bachelor of Education (class-teacher system)
- Bachelor of Physical Education
- Bachelor's degrees in specialized courses such as Arabic, English, chemistry, computer science, or history with a minor in education
- Associate Diploma in Early Childhood. (Bahrain, 1996)

The courses and programs deal with modern methods of teaching and learning. In particular, emphasis is placed on the use of educational technology in teaching and learning. Teaching methods covered during teacher education preparation include the discussion, lecture, demonstration, and problem-solving methods. The prospective teachers are also trained to plan lessons to match the cognitive abilities of children. The main goal here is to move away from memorization to strategies the actively engage the student in the learning process (Boyle, 2006).

CLASSROOM MANAGEMENT

Classroom management is based upon modern principles of teaching and learning. The classroom strategies espoused by Dreikurs and Soltz (1990), such as showing respect for students, caring for their needs, including respect for order, avoiding giving undue attention, being firm without dominating, and being flexible, all form part of the teacher education program. So, when teachers enter the classroom, they have a fairly good idea about how to manage the classroom.

Unlike in previous years when memorization was the order of the day in the classroom, teachers today use modern methods of teaching such as group work, projects, and homework. This does not in any way imply that teachers do not use rote methods of learning, however (Boyle, 2006). Memorization is still used in the classroom, especially in mathematics, science, and history classes. Teachers interact with students during the learning process (Cook, 2000).

Teachers have limited authority to discipline students in the classroom. Common disciplinary measures include the teacher asking a student to stand in one corner of the classroom while the teacher continues to teach or adjusting a student's grades for cheating or misbehavior. Students who commit serious offenses are often sent home or expelled from the school.

COEDUCATION

Coeducation is practiced on limited bases in some of the countries, especially at the lower grades and in the private schools. Egypt, Israel, Oman, Syria,

Turkey, and Cyprus have well-developed coeducational institutions in the region. Although both boys and girls may be in the same class, they often sit and work in different parts of the classroom. Girls usually cover their hair with a scarf while in the classroom or at school. This is strictly enforced by the teacher both in and out of the classroom. In the classroom, teachers have to respect this requirement in all public schools.

At the pre-primary school level, coeducation is practiced. Boys and girls study in the same room, play together, and have common interactions at school. Young girls do not have to cover their head or face in the classroom. This is particularly common in Egypt, Iraq, Algeria, Tunisia, Morocco, and the United Arab Emirates. Coeducation is one of the modern trends in education in the region, because tradition in the Arab countries insists on the separation of the sexes for education and other social activities (Qubain, 1966).

REFERENCES

Akkari, A. (2004). Education in the Middle East and North Africa: The current situation and future challenges. *International Education Journal, 5*(2), 144–153.

Arends, R. I. (2004). *Learning to teach* (6th ed.). Boston: McGraw-Hill.

Bahrain. (1996). *Bahrain*. Report presented to the 45th session of the International Conference on Education, Geneva, September 30–October 5. Available at http://www.ibe.unesco.org/countries/countryDossier/natrep96/bahrain96.pdf.

Bahrain Bayan School. (2005). Preschool (Nursery–KG2). http://www.bayanschool.edu.bh/default.asp?action=category&id=38.

Boyle, H. N. (2006). Memorization and learning in Islamic schools. *Comparative Education Review, 50*(3), 478–495.

British International School of Al Khobar. (2006). *Parent-Student Handbook*. Available at http://www.britishschool-ksa.com/handbook/parent-student_handbook_sep_2007.pdf.

Cook, B. J. (2000). Egypt's national education debate. *Comparative Education, 36*(4), 477–490.

Dreikurs, R., & Soltz, V. (1990). *Children: The challenge*. New York: Plume.

El-Tawil, E. A. (1984). The relative effects of certified teachers on their pupils' achievement. *School Psychology International, 5*, 103–106.

Herrera, L. (2003). Participation in school upgrading: Gender, class and (in)action in Egypt. *International Journal of Educational Development, 23*, 187–199.

Israel. (1996). *Israel: National report, 1996*. Report presented to the 45th session of the International Conference on Education, Geneva, September 30–October 5. Available at http://www.ibe.unesco.org/countries/countryDossier/natrep96/israel96.pdf.

Nasser, R. (2004). Exclusion and the making of Jordanian national identity: An analysis of school textbooks. *Nationalism and Ethnic Politics, 10*, 221–249.

Qubain, F. I. (1966). *Education and science in the Arab world*. Baltimore: Johns Hopkins University Press.

UNESCO. Institute for Statistics. (2007). *Education Systems*. Retrieved July 1, 2007. http://stats.uis.unesco.org/unesco/TableViewer/tableView.aspx?ReportId=163.

UNESCO. International Bureau of Education. (2006). *Bahrain*. http://www.ibe.unesco.org/countries/WDE/2006/ARAB_STATES/Bahrain/Bahrain.pdf.

UNESCO. (2006a). Israel: Early childhood care and education (ECCE) programmes. IBE/2006/EFA/GMR/CP/38. Geneva: UNESCO. Available at http://unesdoc. unesco.org/images/0014/001472/147202e.pdf.

———. (2006b). Oman: Early childhood care and education (ECCE) programmes. IBE/2006/EFA/GMR/CP/63. Geneva: UNESCO. Available at http://unesdoc. unesco.org/images/0014/001472/147202e.pdf.

UNESCO. International Bureau of Education. (2006). *Bahrain.* http://www.ibe. unesco.org/countries/WDE/2006/ARAB_STATES/Bahrain/Bahrain.pdf.

———. (2006). *United Arab Emirates.* http://www.ibe.unesco.org/countries/WDE/ 2006/ARAB_STATES/United_Arab_Emirates/United_Arab_Emirates.pdf.

———. (2006). *World Data on Education,* 6th Ed. http://www.ibe.unesco.org/ countries/WDE/2006/ARAB_STATES/Jordan/Jordan.pdf.

Chapter 5

HIGHER EDUCATION IN THE MIDDLE EAST AND NORTH AFRICA

The development of modern higher education institutions started in the Middle East and North Africa before the intrusions of Europeans in the region (Lulat, 2005; Mizikaci, 2006). Al-Azhar mosque, built in 972 CE, for more than a thousand years served as one of the main institutions of higher learning in the Middle East and North Africa. Students from all over the Islamic world flocked to Cairo to study at Al-Azhar University. The curriculum included religious and as well as secular subjects.

However, the foundations of the modern higher education system were laid by Great Britain and France, although European nations such as Italy and Greece had also in the past played a significant role in the development of education in the region. The British and French efforts in the region were often geared toward the development of elementary and secondary education. The United States, however, played a significant role in the development of higher education in the Middle Eastern and North African (MENA) countries, especially in Egypt, Iraq, and Lebanon. The American University in Cairo, St. Joseph University, Beirut College for Women in Lebanon, Al-Hakima University of Baghdad, and the American University of Beirut are all examples of the involvement of the United States in the development and promotion of higher education in the region (Faksh, 1976).

The main problem with the development of higher education during the colonial era was that progress was slow. Higher education is an expensive enterprise, and so the colonial powers did not want to invest a lot of resources in its development. The few universities and colleges in the region during the colonial period could not cater for the needs of all students, and therefore many students seeking higher education credentials had to travel overseas, especially to France or the United Kingdom. For instance, in 1826, Egypt sent forty-four students to France to study various courses. Some of the students studied courses in civil and military administration; others studied medicine and agriculture (Heyworth-Dunne, 1938). This trend continued throughout the colonial period.

When each country gained independence, education became one of the areas that the new government saw the need to develop. Each government introduced several measures to make elementary education free and compulsory. In the more affluent countries like Kuwait, higher education was also made free. In some of the countries, students are now provided "monthly allowance, uniforms, books, transportation, and other necessities" (Bahgat, 1999, p. 130).

Governments in the MENA region paid attention to the development of higher education for several reasons:

- Faculty and students in universities often conduct research into problems to find solutions that benefit society as a whole.
- Higher education institutions train people in highly desirable skills required for industrial and technological development.
- Higher education institutions provide people with high-level knowledge in social, political, and economic affairs.
- Higher education institutions provide room for high school students who want to acquire higher education skills.
- Higher education institutions provide opportunities for countries to be self-reliant in training skilled labor for the local economy.

In the sections that follow, the development, progress, and status of higher education in the region will be discussed with reference to selected countries.

PRIVATE HIGHER EDUCATION

A new trend that is shaping the development of higher education in the MENA region is the involvement of the private sector. For more than a century, the provision of higher education in the region was the sole responsibility of the individual governments. However, the United States during the early part of the nineteenth century established universities and colleges in Egypt and Lebanon. The American University in Cairo was founded in 1919 by Americans who were interested in making higher education accessible and affordable to people in Egypt and surrounding countries. The American University in Beirut, founded in 1866 by an independent body of educators from the United States, is a non-sectarian higher education institution designed to promote learning for students in Lebanon and the other countries in the region.

After the 1980s, each government introduced legislation that made it possible for the private sector to enter into the development of higher education. Article 19 of the laws governing private education in Bahrain states:

1. A private educational or training institution may not effect any change or alteration to the prescribed educational or training curricula except after securing the Ministry's approval.

2. The Ministry shall change or suspend any curricula, books, or programs that are inconsistent with the State's policy and the laws in force in the country and the implementing regulations thereof. (Bahrain, Ministry of Education, 2007)

As a result of the involvement of the private sector in the development and organization of higher education in the region, Egypt and Lebanon now each have more than ten private universities and colleges, and Tunisia has over ten.

HIGHER EDUCATION IN BAHRAIN

Higher education in Bahrain is provided by public as well as private institutions. Public institutions include the Arabian Gulf University, AMA International University, Arab Open University (Bahrain Branch), University College of Bahrain, and the University of Bahrain. Ahlia University was the first private higher education institution established in Bahrain. The school cycle for higher education begins in October and ends in August.

Admission Requirements

Admission to higher education in Bahrain is open to both men and women. Admission requirements differ from institution to institution. However, in all the universities in Bahrain, the minimum admission requirements for university education include high school graduation with a good pass. Below are the admission requirements for the Gulf University, where students may enroll to complete a bachelor's, master's, or doctoral program:

- For a bachelor's degree: Direct-entry applicants must have a high school educational background.
- For a master's degree: Applicants must have a bachelor's degree.
- For a doctoral degree: Applicants must have a master's degree.
- For the University of London Program: Students should obtain a TOEFL (Test of English as a Foreign Language) score of 550 (250 computer) or better by the end of the preparatory year at Gulf University.
- Students are required to be fluent in Arabic or English.
- Foreign students must have visas and must be able to pay full fees unless they have a scholarship.

Programs of Study

Graduate programs available in Bahrain include:

- Business administration
- Education: learning disabilities, intellectual disabilities and autistic disorder, and distance learning and training
- Technology, in particular biotechnology

- Technology management
- Environmental management
- Desert and arid zone sciences
- Geographic information system (GIS) remote sensing
- Environmental sciences and natural resources
- Desert farming and soilless agriculture
- Medicine and medical sciences

Undergraduate programs include Business Administration, Information Technology, Media and Communication, and Nursing.

Enrollment

Enrollment in higher education institutions in Bahrain is substantial. It is the objective of most of the students in the region to get a higher degree in science, business, or technology, which is an assurance of a good job and a higher social status.

Grading

The grading system used in Bahrain's universities is shown in table 5.1.

Table 5.1
Main Grading System Used by Higher Education Institutions in Bahrain

Grade	Comments
A or 4	Excellent
B, B+, or 3	Good
C, C+, or 2	Satisfactory
D, D+, or 1	Minimum pass
F or 0	Fail

Ahlia University, Manama, Bahrain

Ahlia University is a private higher education institution. It was established in 2001 following the granting of license by the government of Bahrain. All the programs offered are approved by the Bahraini government. The university has four colleges:

- The College of Mathematical Sciences and Information Technology, which offers bachelor's degrees in Information Technology, Internet Science and Technology, and Mobile Phone Technology and Computing and a master's degree in Information Technology

- The College of Banking and Finance, which offers bachelor's degrees in Accounting and Finance, Banking and Finance, Management Information Systems, Marketing and Management, and Economics and Finance and a Master's in Business Administration (MBA)
- The College of Medical and Health Sciences, a relatively new department that currently offers only a bachelor's degree in Physiotherapy
- The College of Arts and Fine Arts, which offers bachelor's degrees in Interior Design and Graphic Design and both bachelor's and master's degrees in Mass Communication and Public Relations

These programs offer students in the region the opportunity to get quality education without traveling far from home.

HIGHER EDUCATION IN EGYPT

Egypt has more than fifty institutions of higher learning. These are provided by the government as well as by foreign nations and the private sector. The foreign nations that established schools include the United States, France, the United Kingdom, and Germany. The first university opened in the country is Al-Azhar. Opened in 972 CE by religious leaders to offer education to the public, it was converted to a university in 1061. The first secular university in the country is Cairo University.

Colleges and universities in Egypt include:

- Ain Shams University
- Al-Azhar University
- Alexandria University
- Al-Fayoum University
- American University in Cairo
- Arab Academy for Science, Technology, and Maritime Transport
- Arab Open University (Egypt Branch)
- Assiut University
- Banha University
- Beni-Suef University
- Cairo University
- French University of Egypt
- German University in Cairo
- Helwan University Cairo
- Higher Institute of Technology–Benha
- Kafr El-Sheikh University
- Mansoura University
- Minia University
- Minufiya University
- Misr International University
- Misr University for Science and Technology
- Modern Science and Arts University

- October 6 University
- Senghor University
- Sohag University
- South Valley University
- Suez Canal University
- Tanta University
- Zagazig University

Admission Requirements

The numerous higher education institutions in Egypt have different admission requirements for the various academic programs. These also differ by level of education. In general, students seeking admission to any of the degree-granting institutions should have a secondary school certificate (*Thanawya Amma*) or its equivalent. International students should also possess a valid visa. Students should be fluent in Arabic, English, French, or German. Students seeking master's or doctoral degrees need to present their first university degree and attend an interview and other requirements set by a particular institution. Some institutions place a cap on the number of students they admit each year, and some administer their own entrance examinations (Salmi, 1999).

Credentials Conferred

Degrees offered by Egyptian higher education institutions include bachelor's, master's, and doctoral degrees. Some programs confer nondegree credentials such as certificates or diplomas.

Programs of Study

Egyptian institutions of higher learning offer many majors, including:

- African Studies
- Agriculture
- Arts
- Business
- Commerce
- Computer Science and Information Systems
- Dentistry
- Education
- Engineering
- Fine Arts
- Languages
- Law
- Medicine
- Nursing
- Pharmacy

Table 5.2
Enrollment at Ain Shams University, Egypt, 2004/2005

Department/Faculty	Male	Female	Total
Arts	5,435	20,595	26,030
Law	14,330	12,019	26,349
Commerce	27,930	18,560	46,490
Science	2,283	2,752	5,035
Engineering	8,533	2,719	11,252
Medicine	4,527	4,323	8,850
Agriculture	953	1,077	2,030
Education	3,846	11,114	14,960
Women	—	15,881	15,881
Pharmacy	911	1,600	2,511
Dentistry	556	840	1,396
Computer & Information	562	519	1,081
Specific Education	568	1475	2,043
Nursing	—	962	962
Total	*101,047*	*72,081*	*173,128*
	(58%)	*(42%)*	

Source: Ain Shams University (2007).

- Physical Education
- Science
- Social Sciences

Enrollment

Enrollment in colleges and universities in Egypt is high because credentials in higher education are an essential prerequisite for procurement of high-paying jobs. Again, it is a reflection of high social status. Table 5.2 shows the enrollment breakdown for Aim Shams University for the 2004/2005 academic year. It is interesting to note that 58 percent of the students enrolled are women. Significantly, more females than males are enrolled in science-related courses, agriculture, and pharmacy; these are encouraging indicators for changes in the patterns of gender roles and education, because these disciplines are generally believed to be male-dominated professions. On the other hand, no males are enrolled in nursing, because it is considered a female profession here, as in many parts of the world.

From table 5.3, it appears that most students enroll in Commerce (11,249 students). This two-year diploma certificate is necessary for people who want to seek jobs in industry, commerce, business administration, and education. At this same level of the educational ladder, Education comes next in popularity (2,100 students). This certificate is essential for people seeking employment in the field of education as administrators or teachers.

Table 5.3
Number of Postgraduate Students at Ain Shams University, 2004/2005

Faculty/Department	Diploma	Master's	Doctorate
Law	1,841	—	34
Commerce	11,249	265	189
Science	192	13	11
Engineering	235	1,729	297
Medicine	447	1,405	50
Agriculture	54	501	335
Education	2,100	707	259
Women	428	487	323
Al-Alsun	45	185	82
Pharmacy	—	66	1
Dentistry	98	37	36
Computer & Information	—	—	3
Specific Education	210	129	108
Nursing	63	—	19
Childhood Studies	—	353	255
Environmental Studies	106	962	34
Total	*17,535*	*6,406*	*2,185*

Source: Ain Shams University (2007).

The most popular course at the master's level is Engineering, followed closely by Medicine. These two areas are very popular because students graduating in these areas are in high demand in the region.

At the doctoral level, the number of students enrolled keeps dwindling. Fewer students continue on to doctoral studies after the master's program because most of them find lucrative jobs with the master's degree. However, Agriculture is the most popular program at the doctoral level, followed by Women's Studies.

Grading Systems

The basic grading system used by Egypt's higher education institutions is shown in table 5.4.

HIGHER EDUCATION IN SYRIA

In Syria, as in the other countries in the Middle East and North Africa, students enroll in universities, colleges, and institutes for higher education credentials. The Ministry of Education is responsible for the establishment of higher education. The minister of higher education is responsible for the implementation of these programs.

Table 5.4
Main Grading System Used by Higher Education Institutions in Egypt

Grade	Comments
75–100	Distinguished, Excellent
65–74	Good
50–64	Pass
0–49	Poor

Universities in Syria

Syria has a number of excellent universities and educational facilities. There are several universities in Syria, the largest being Damascus University, followed by the University of Aleppo. Other universities include Tishreen University, Al-Bath University, the University of Damascus, Arab European University (AEU), International University for Science and Technology, Wadi German Syrian University (WGSU), Syrian Virtual University, the Higher Institute of Business Administration, and the Higher Institute of Applied Sciences (HIAST). These institutions offer various degrees in Agriculture, Architecture, Medicine, Law, Science, Engineering, Liberal Arts, Business, Education, and Computer Science.

Admission Policies

Requirements for admission into Syrian higher education institutions include a general secondary certificate. Students seeking admission to study Medicine, Engineering, or Law are required by the admission standards to show higher performance on all tests. Education is free at all public institutions at all levels for Syrians.

Foreign students must obtain a valid visa and a residence permit from Syrian embassies abroad before leaving their home countries for Syria. For students whose language proficiency in Arabic is not adequate, each university has a facility to help such students. Students pay fees for this service.

Degrees Offered

The University of Aleppo in Aleppo, Syria, offers bachelor's, master's, and doctoral degrees. The university also offers two-year certificates and diploma courses.

Program of Studies

Today, the University of Aleppo consists of twenty academic faculties, including those in Civil Engineering, Architecture, Mechanical Engineering, Electrical and Electronic Engineering, Informatics, Technological Engineering, Agriculture, Medicine, Sciences, Arts and Humanities, Economics, Dentistry, Pharmacy, Law, Education, and Agriculture Sciences. The Institute for the History of Arabic Science awards diploma, master's, and Ph.D. degrees in Basic, Medical, and Applied Sciences and Archaeology.

Scholarly Journals and Periodicals Published by University of Aleppo

The following journals and periodicals are issued by Aleppo University Press (University of Aleppo, 2007):

- *Arts and Humanities*
- *Agricultural Sciences*
- *Medical Sciences*
- *Basic Sciences*
- *Engineering Sciences*
- *Economical Sciences*
- *Journal for the History of Arabic Science*
- *Newsletter of the Institute for the History of Arabic Science*
- *Aleppo's Adiyat* (yearly)
- *Aleppo University Prospectus*
- *Cosmic Technologies* (issued by the Faculty of Informatics)

Every year, university faculty and students publish a number of articles in these periodicals. The articles include topics of general interest from engineering to social science.

Enrollment

The University of Aleppo had 61,643 students at all faculties and departments during the 2004/2005 academic year. There were 11,184 students at institutes and 26,707 at the Open University Education Center. That year, the university had 1,096 Arab and foreign students and 1,525 postgraduate students (University of Aleppo, 2007).

Libraries

Each faculty or academic department at the University of Aleppo has a library. These libraries work as subsidiaries of the Central Library, which houses about 509,000 reference volumes and numerous magazines, newsletters, and pamphlets. The library was built in 1980 to hold about a million books. It is designed to accommodate more than 15,000 students.

University libraries subscribe to more than 325 periodicals in various subjects and languages. The Central Library supervises the branch libraries of academic faculties, institutes, learning centers, the Institute of Languages, and university hospitals. It supplies them with books, periodicals, and journals.

HIGHER EDUCATION IN MOROCCO

The higher education system in Morocco follows the French system. This is not strange because of the influence the French had on the education in the country during the colonial era. At present, Morocco has more than sixty higher education institutions ranging from colleges to universities and institutes. The institutes offer two-year certificate or diploma degrees; the universities offer bachelor's, master's and doctoral studies. There are private as well as public institutions of higher learning.

Enrollment in higher education institutions in Morocco continues to soar. In the 1997/1998 academic year, students in higher education totaled 243,000. By 1999/2000, it had increased to 251,000. This trend has been made possible by the interest the Moroccan government has shown in developing higher education institutions in the country. Table 5.5 lists the enrollment of students at some of the universities in Morocco for 1998/1999.

Table 5.5
Student Enrollment and Staff Size at Universities in Morocco, 1998/1999

University (Location)	Institutions	Student Enrollment		Staff	
		Total	Female	Total	Female
Mohamed V Soussi (Rabat)	5	14,155	6,584	902	268
Mohamed V Agdal (Rabat)	5	23,944	11,458	1,184	325
Sidi Mohamed Ben Abdallah (Fez)	7	26,701	10,328	1,021	201
Qarawyin (Fez)	4	5,968	2,057	126	12
Mohamed I (Oujda)	4	19,246	8,432	589	76
Qadi Ayiad (Marrakesh)	8	32,414	11,955	1,251	232
Hassan II Ain Chock (Casablanca)	7	29,202	14,526	1,203	362
Hassan II (Mohammedia)	5	16,312	7,967	721	213
Ibn Tofail (Kenitra)	2	7,894	3,658	402	127
Abdelmalek Saadi (Tetuan)	6	9,929	4,683	550	101
Moulay Ismail (Meknes)	6	22,003	8,412	651	118
Ibn Zohr (Agadir)	4	11,205	3,982	451	87
Chouaib Doukkali (El Jadida)	2	7,796	3,562	440	97
Hassan I (Settat)	3	3,135	1,278	176	55
Total	68	229,904	98,882	9,667	2,274

Source: Ouakrime (2007).

Admission Policies

Like the other institutions of higher learning in the region, students wishing to enter any of Morocco's universities or institutes must have a secondary school leaving certificate or its equivalent and must pass entrance exams in some cases (such as for Medicine, Pharmacy, and Dentistry). A good knowledge of Arabic or French is required, and English is required for students wishing to study the English language. Foreign students must obtain valid visas from the Moroccan Embassy before leaving their home country to study in Morocco.

Students who have completed their bachelor's program and have relevant work experience are eligible to apply for admission to a master's program. Such students may have to pass an entrance examination administered by the institution. Students wishing to enter a doctoral program need to have completed their master's program.

Grading System

Moroccan universities use a 20-point grading system (see table 5.6). Any score over 10 is considered a pass. Students must pass above 50 percent on the end-of-year written and oral examination to move on to the next stage of the academic program (Clark, 2006).

Al Akhawayn University, Ifrane, Morocco

Al Akhawayn University was established in 1993 by a royal charter. It started operating as a small private university in January 1995. Al Akhawayn is a coeducational institution and is designed along the American model of higher education. English is used as the main language of instruction, although Arabic

Table 5.6
Grading System Used by Higher Education Institutions in Morocco

Scale	Grade Description	U.S. Grade Equivalent
15+	Très Bien (Very Good)	A+
13–14.9	Bien (Good)	A
12–12.9	Assez Bien (Quite Good)	B+
11–11.9	Passable (Satisfactory)	B
10–10.9	Moyen (Sufficient)	C
8–9.9	—	*

* May be considered a passing grade if the entire year is passed.
Source: Clark (2006).

and French are used in some classes. It offers both undergraduate and graduate programs in several academic areas, including:

- Business Administration
- Humanities and Social Sciences
- Islamic Culture and Arts
- Language
- Natural Resources
- Science and Engineering
- Strategic Studies

Admission

The admission of students for undergraduate studies depends upon:

- Evaluation of secondary school grades
- Success in the General Admission Test, GAT or an SAT score of 1000
- Placement Tests in Arabic, French, and English Writing, where applicable
- Satisfactory interview, where applicable. (Al Akhawayn University, 2005a, p. 34)

To get into a graduate program, the basic requirements for acceptance are:

- A bachelor degree from an accredited institution, or equivalent (e.g., a Moroccan License);
- Strong academic average in course work leading to the License; or, if graduating from a system using the U.S. higher education model, a "B" average or better in upper level (junior and senior level) work and in any graduate work already completed; or, other evidence of ability to succeed in graduate study;
- Adequate preparation for the proposed graduate program; and, acceptance by the appropriate Admissions Committee.

Selected candidates may be invited to take an interview with the admissions committee.

All graduate students, wishing ... to pursue a master's degree are expected to demonstrate proficiency in the English language. For placement purposes, students for whom English is not the first language must submit a TOEFL score of 550 and obtain a 5.0 score over 6.0 in Writing. (Al Akhawayn University, 2005a, p. 39)

Library

The main library at Al Akhawayn University is the Mohammed IV Library. It contains more than 70,000 books, periodicals, monographs, and magazines. In 2004, the library acquired more than 8,000 monographs and 8,063 books (Al Akhawayn University, 2005b).

The library has access to Academic Search Premier, Business Source Premier, Econlit, Eric, MEDLINE, and Regional Business News. These are all powerful databases used by many academic institutions all over the world to conduct research. Between February and May 2005, the database most frequently used by students for research was Academic Search Premier, followed by Business Source Premier.

Additional resources available at the library include digital cameras; access to an intranet and the Internet; the World Bank Public Information Center; multimedia items such as CDs, DVDs, televisions, and video projectors; scanners; laptop and desktop computers; and the Multimedia Information Center.

HIGHER EDUCATION IN SAUDI ARABIA

Saudi Arabia is one of the countries in the Middle East and North Africa that has made significant and tremendous progress in the development of higher education. The main objective for the development and promotion of higher education in Saudi Arabia is to train Saudi citizens to lead the nation in development. To this end, no stone has been left unturned in the government's efforts to make higher education available and affordable to all qualified citizens.

Higher education is offered at universities, girls' colleges, and higher training institutes. Progress has been made possible largely as a result of the large revenues the country earns from the oil industry. The development of higher education in the country started in 1957 with the establishment of King Saud University in Riyadh (Saleh, 1986). The university initially had twenty-one students and nine teachers. By the close of the 1969/1970 academic year, enrollment had jumped to 2,899 students.

Saudi Arabia continued to open new universities to meet the demand of the teeming population. By the end of the 1981/1982 academic year, Saudi Arabia had established nine colleges and universities with a total student population of 63,563 and a staff of 6,906 teachers (Saleh, 1986). These institutions included King Abdul Aziz University, King Faisal University, Umm al-Qura University, Dar al-Hekma College, and Islamic University (Saudi Arabia, Ministry of Education, 2003).

The kingdom now has seven principal universities:

- King Saud University in Riyadh, established in 1957
- Islamic University in Medina, established in 1961
- King Abdul Aziz University in Jeddah, established in 1967
- Imam Mohammed bin Saud Islamic University in Riyadh, established in 1953 (it acquired university status in 1974)
- King Faisal University in Dammam and Hafouf, established in 1975
- King Fahd University for Oil and Minerals in Dhahran, established in 1963 as the University for Oil and Minerals (acquired university status in 1975)
- Umm al-Qura University in Mecca, established in 1979

Saudi women generally receive higher education in separate women's institutions that offer four-year bachelor's, master's, and doctoral degrees (Saleh, 1986). Higher educational institutions for women include:

- College of Arts (Riyadh)
- College of Arts (Dammam)
- College of Education (Riyadh)
- College of Education (Jeddah)
- College of Education (Mecca)
- College of Education (Abha)
- College of Education (Buraidah)
- College of Education (Medina)
- College of Education (Tabuk)
- College of Education (Dammam)
- College of Social Work (Riyadh)

In Saudi Arabia, the provision of higher education is the responsibility of the Ministry of Higher Education. This department was established in 1975 to offer supervision for university education and other higher institutions in the country. The Islamic University of Medina is administered by a Council of Ministers. The Ministry of Education also supervises teachers' colleges as well as colleges for women (Saudi Arabia, Ministry of Education, 2003).

Admission to Higher Education

Students admitted to higher education institutions in Saudi Arabia must possess the General Secondary Education Certificate Examination (*Tawjihi*). Individual faculties may administer their own entrance exam in addition to the Tawjihi. Students wishing to enroll in nonuniversity higher education need to present a General Secondary Certificate (Sciences Stream), a Secondary Vocational Diploma, or a Secondary Commercial School Diploma (Sedgwick, 2001).

Admission of Foreign Students

Undergraduate admission requirements for foreign students include holding a qualification equivalent to the General Secondary Education (Tawjihi with required pass mark). A bachelor's degree is required to enter a master's program, and a master's degree for doctoral studies. Some departments or faculties may require entrance examinations and interviews or letters of recommendations from foreign students. Students must also hold a visa and have a good knowledge of Arabic. Students wishing to study in the University of Petroleum and Minerals must be fluent in English.

King Saud University

King Saud University was established in 1957 to train personnel to contribute to the economic and social development of the country. Among other things, the university was founded to:

- provide instruction in Islamic studies, arts and sciences, and specialized fields
- train teachers
- promote the acquisition of knowledge through encouraging scientific research
- develop the right university spirit among students
- promote sporting, social, artistic, and cultural life for students
- organize students' leisure time so as to be useful to them and the country
- offer a comfortable environment for students inside and outside the university conducive for their personal and professional growth. (Saleh, 1986; Bahgat, 1999)

Admissions Procedures

Entry into a bachelor's program at King Saud University requires a recent high school certificate from a Saudi school or an equivalent certificate and a grade average of 90 percent. Candidates may be asked to take a qualifying test at some of the departments. For master's programs, a bachelor's degree from King Saud University or an equivalent degree is needed, along with an interview or admission test. Doctoral programs require a master's or equivalent degree from King Saud University or another recognized university or academic institution. Individual departments may require additional documents and a qualifying interview.

Enrollment

Table 5.7 shows the number of students enrolled in various different postgraduate programs at King Saud University during the 2004/2005 academic year.

Libraries

King Saud University has a library complex with seven libraries in addition to the central library, the Prince Salman Central Library. The library complex provides academic services to the general student body, including photocopying, Internet services, lending, and computer database searches. It also provides other services such as book fairs for students and the general public. The library has more than two million volumes (King Saud University, 2007).

INTERNATIONAL EDUCATION

Students studying in the Middle East and North Africa may participate in international education programs. These include programs that take students to other countries within the region. Also, there are study abroad programs that take students outside the region to countries such as the United Kingdom and the United States (Mizikaci, 2006).

Table 5.7
Postgraduate Enrollment at King Saud University, 2004/2005

Program	Number of Students Enrolled
Arts	641
Education	989
Food Sciences & Agriculture	244
Pharmacy	99
Medicine	8
Dentistry	34
Sciences	621
Administrative Sciences	592
Computer & Information Science	175
Applied Medical Sciences	72
Architecture & Planning	157
Engineering	333
Total	*3,965*

Source: King Saud University (2007).

Within the region, Egypt has served as a destination for thousands of students from the other MENA countries. Syria upon the attainment of independence established an education system that followed the Egyptian model. Today, other countries such as Bahrain, Saudi Arabia, and Kuwait all attract Middle Eastern and North African students to study in their education institutions.

Turkey for many years has been sending students abroad to study various subjects in computer science, engineering, education, and mathematics. Table 5.8 shows where these students were studying in 2000.

Students going to school in Bahrain get the opportunity to participate in international education. For example, during the 2000/2001 academic year, Bahrain sent more than six hundred students to study in other countries in the region. Of these, 19 studied in Oman, 106 in the United Arab Emirates, 105 in Qatar, 162 in Kuwait, 118 in Saudi Arabia, and 194 in Egypt. During the same academic year, Bahrain sent another three hundred students abroad to study in countries outside the MENA countries. India attracted 182 of these students, the United Kingdom took 112, and the United States, 63 (Bahrain, Ministry of Education, 2007)

Some of the courses the Bahraini students studied abroad included:

- Commercial and Business Administration, mostly in India
- Education Science, mostly in the United Kingdom
- Engineering, mostly in the United States
- Law and Sharia, mostly in Egypt
- Mathematics, Statistics, and Computer Science, mostly in the United Arab Emirates and Saudi Arabia

Table 5.8
Turkish Students Abroad, 2000

Country of destination	Percentage
Australia	0.6
Austria	3.2
Belgium	0.9
Denmark	0.3
Finland	0.1
France	4.6
Germany	57.3
Greece	0.1
Hungary	0.1
Italy	0.2
Japan	0.2
Netherlands	1.9
Norway	0.1
Sweden	0.3
Switzerland	1.3
United Kingdom	3.0
United States	25.5

Source: OECD (2004).

HIGHER EDUCATION IN ISRAEL

The first institution of higher learning, Technion-Israel Institute of Technology was founded in 1912 and started enrolling students in 1924, twenty-four years before the founding of the State of Israel. The successful operation of Technion-Israel led to the establishment of another institution, Hebrew University of Jerusalem, which was founded in 1918 and opened in 1925 as a university. A third university that was founded before the independence of Israel in 1948 was the Weizmann Institute of Science in Rehovot. It was founded in 1934 to provide science and technology education to male and female Jewish students.

In Israel, higher education is divided into three main categories. There are universities and institutes that offer doctoral and degree programs; academic and regional colleges that offer undergraduate programs; and teacher training colleges that grant undergraduate degrees in education.

The universities and institutes include:

- Bar-Ilan University in Ramat-Gan
- Ben Gurion University of the Negev in Beer-Sheva
- Open University, in Tel Aviv
- Tel Aviv University in Tel Aviv
- University of Haifa, in Haifa. (Beller, 2001)

The academic and regional colleges include:

- Academic College of Law, Ramat Gan
- Academic College of Tel Aviv-Jaffa, Tel Aviv
- Afeka-Tel Aviv Academic College of Engineering, Tel Aviv
- Ariel University Center of Samaria, Ariel
- Ashkelon Academic College, Ashkelon
- Bezalel Academy of Arts and Design, Jerusalem
- College of Management, Rishon LeZion
- Hadassah College, Jerusalem
- Holon Institute of Technology, Holon
- Interdisciplinary Center, Herliya
- Jerusalem Academy of Music and Dance, Jerusalem
- Jerusalem College of Engineering, Jerusalem
- Jerusalem College of Technology (Machon Lev), Jerusalem
- Kinneret Academic College, Jordan Valley
- Lander Institute, Jerusalem
- Netanya Academic College, Netanya
- Ono Academic College, Kiryat Ono
- Ort Braude College, Karmiel
- Ruppin College, Emek Hefer
- Sapir Academic College, Hof Ashkelon
- Shaarey Mishpat College of Law, Hod HaSharon
- Shamoon College of Engineering, Beer-Sheva
- Shenkar College of Engineering and Design, Ramat Gan
- Technological College of Beer Sheva, Beer Sheva
- Tel-Hai College, Tel-Hai
- Touro College, Jerusalem
- Western Galilee College, Acre
- Yehuda Regional College, Kiryat Arba
- Yizrael Valley College, Emek Yizrael
- Zefat College, Zefat
- Zinman College for Physical Education and Sports. (Wingate Institute, Netanya)

Teacher Training Colleges include

- Achva College of Education, Beer-Tuvia
- Arab College for Education, Haifa
- Beit Berl College, Beit Berl
- College of Technology Education, Tel Aviv
- David Yellin College of Education, Jerusalem
- Efrata College of Education, Jerusalem
- Emuna College of Education, Jerusalem
- Givat Washington College of Education, Jerusalem
- Gordon College of Education, Haifa
- Hemdat College of Education, Netivot
- Herzog Teacher's College at Yeshivat Har Etzion, Alon Shvut

- Jerusalem College Michlala, Jerusalem
- Kaye College of Education, Beer-Sheva
- Kibbutzim College of Education, Tel Aviv
- Levinsky College of Education, Tel Aviv
- Lifsihz Religious College of Education, Jerusalem
- Mofet Consortium of Colleges of Education, Tel Aviv
- Moreshet Yaakov Religious College of Education, Rehovot
- Ohalo College of Education, Katzrin
- Oranim Academic College of Education, Tivon
- Orot College for Women, Elkana
- Ort College for Teachers of Technology, Tel Aviv
- Shaanan Religious College of Education, Haifa
- Talpiot College of Education, Tel Aviv
- Wizo College of Design and Education, Haifa. (Israel Science and Technology, 2008)

By law, higher education institutions are autonomous. The licensing and accrediting body is the Council for Higher Education (Sprinzak, Sergev, Bar, & Leve-Mazloum, 1996). The main functions of the Council for Higher Education include:

- Submitting higher education budget to the government
- Safeguarding academic freedom
- Allocating budgets to approved higher education institutions
- Expressing its opinion on all matters concerning higher education
- Promoting efficiency in higher education through its accreditation procedures. (UNESCO, 2008)

Admission Requirements

Different higher education institutions may require different education credentials in order to offer admission to a student. However, for a bachelor's degree, students seeking admission must possess an advanced degree certificate called *Bagrut* or its equivalent. Some universities may require entrance examinations and interview (Beller, 2001). A bachelor's degree is required for students seeking to enter a master's degree program or its equivalent. Some universities may require an entrance examination, interview, and other credentials. International students should possess a valid visa. Knowledge in Hebrew, Arabic, and English is a plus. Students applying for doctoral studies should have completed a master's degree or equivalent credentials.

Programs and Degrees

Israeli higher education systems offer bachelor's, master's, and doctoral degrees in various academic disciplines. The bachelor's degree is conferred on successful candidates after four years of studies, except in the sciences, especially pharmacy, medicine, and engineering, where students may spend at least five years. Students accumulate a minimum of forty semester hours.

Students may obtain a bachelor's degree in accounting, agriculture, Arabic, archaeology, architecture, biology, business, computer science, economics, education, engineering, finance, fine art, geography, history, sociology, political science, psychology, marketing, medical laboratory technology, Middle Eastern studies, music, public administration, social work, statistics, mathematics, school system administration, video and video art, or many other areas.

Students obtain a master's degree after two years of studies. Students are required to complete a certain amount of coursework and also complete a dissertation. Apart from the above courses, students may obtain a master's degree in dentistry or business administration.

Students obtain a doctor of philosophy (Ph.D.) degree after three years of studies following successful completion of a master's degree. Like the master's degree, students are required to complete a certain number of courses and a dissertation. The number of courses and years differ from program to program. Generally, students pursuing doctoral studies in sciences such as Doctor of Medicine (M.D) stay in school longer than those seeking doctoral studies in the social sciences.

Enrollment Trends

Enrollments in Israeli institutions of higher learning have been on the rise since the founding of the State of Israel in 1948. Enrollment rates have gone up because the diverse immigrants entering Israel need to acquire skills that will make them highly marketable in the country. To this end, both men and women have been enrolling in science, technology, and social science programs to acquire new skills that are in high demand in the country.

Grading System

Main grading system used by higher education institutions:

Full Description: 100–0
Highest on scale: 100
Pass/fail level: 60, 55, or 50
Lowest on scale: 0

Tel Aviv University: A Short History

The origin of Tel Aviv University goes back to 1956 when Tel Aviv School of Law and Economics, the Institute of Natural Sciences, and the Institute of Jewish Studies joined together to form Tel Aviv University. It is the largest university in Israel today and is a major institution for teaching and research. Tel Aviv University has nine faculties. These include:

- Yolanda and David Katz Faculty of the Arts
- Iby and Aladar Fleischman Faculty of Engineering
- Raymond and Beverly Sackler Faculty of Exact Sciences
- Lester and Sally Entin Faculty of Humanities
- Buchmann Faculty of Law
- George S. Wise Faculty of Life Sciences
- Faculty of Management—Leon Recanati Graduate School of Business Administration
- Sackler Faculty of Medicine
- Gershon H. Gordon Faculty of Social Sciences

It is also of interest to note that Tel Aviv University has several schools where special programs are carried out. These schools include:

- Maurice and Gabriela Goldschleger School of Dental Medicine
- Jaime and Joan Constantiner School of Education
- Porter School of Environmental Studies
- Bob Shapell School of Social Work
- Caesarea–Rothschild School of Communication

Tel Aviv University has over ninety research institutes. These research institutes are generally not independent. They are attached to the other departments and faculties such as science, engineering, agriculture, medicine, and social sciences. This arrangement enables faculty to combine teaching with research. Research forms part of the mission of the university and so faculty are given encouragement, support, and grants to conduct research into issues that affect humanity. Israel has become famous the world over because of its research into social problems, especially agriculture, science, and technology. Israel is located in what is essentially a desert region, but because of its extensive research in agriculture, it is able to produce sufficient food to support its people. Some of the research institutes include:

- Institute for German History
- Institute for Latin American History and Culture
- Jaffee Center for Strategic Studies
- Katz Institute for Research in Hebrew Literature

Undergraduate Studies Admissions

To be eligible for admission to undergraduate programs, candidates must hold a matriculation certificate issued by the Israeli Ministry of Education or an equivalent certificate from abroad. This is called Bagrut. Diplomas such as the French Baccalaureate, German Abitur, British General Certificate of Education (advanced level), and I.B. (International Baccalaureate), and others are equivalent to the Israeli matriculation for registration.

Most students who do not meet all the requirements complete a one year program, the Mechina, where they are given courses in exact sciences, life sciences, social sciences, and the humanities. The main goal of this one year program is to prepare students for higher education in Israel. Fluency in the Hebrew language is required, since the language of instruction is in Hebrew.

Graduate Admissions

Students seeking to complete graduate programs at Tel Aviv University should have a bachelor's degree from an accredited institution and knowledge of Hebrew and English languages. (Some departments may also have other requirements for prospective candidates to meet.)

Degrees Offered

Tel Aviv University offers a number of degrees and diplomas including certificates, bachelors, masters, and doctoral degrees. These certificates, diplomas, and degrees are offered in several academic disciplines.

Library

Tel Aviv University has five main libraries. These include the Brender-Moss Library for Social Sciences and Management; the David J. Light Law Library; the Elias Sourasky Central Library for the Humanities and Arts; the Gitter-Smolarz Library of Life Sciences and Medicine; and the Neiman Library of Exact Sciences and Engineering. Aside from these, each major academic department has its own library. The departmental libraries include the following:

- Archaeology Department
- The Bob Shapell School of Social Work Library
- The Constantiner School of Education Library
- The David Azrieli School of Architecture Library
- The Geographical Library
- The Library of Communication Disorders
- The Mark N. Grinsten Music Library
- The Mehlmann Library
- The Moshi Dayan Center for Middle Eastern and African Studies Library

The universities provide numerous services to students, faculty, and others authorized to use books and materials from the libraries at the university. The services include interlibrary loan, photocopy, e-mail, database services, wireless access, printing, scanning, locker rental, online information retrieval services, and electronic journals and publications. The library has over 300,000 volumes, monographs, and periodicals.

International Studies at Tel Aviv University

Tel Aviv University has established the Overseas Student Program (OSP) where students outside the country may enroll to complete various undergraduate and graduate programs. Program components include Jewish studies, Israel studies, Middle Eastern studies, art studies, Hebrew language studies, and life sciences. The duration for the courses varies from program to program. Some of the courses may last as long as a year. Others are offered only during summer. Tel Aviv University has Overseas Student Program offices in New York, United States; Toorak, Australia; and Toronto, Canada (Tel Aviv University, 2008).

SUMMARY

The Middle East and North Africa have the reputation of being pioneers in the development of higher education. Egypt, Morocco, and Turkey all share the distinction of being leaders in the development of higher education in the region. Since the founding of the University of Constantinople (Fifth century), University of Qarawyin University, in Fez, Morocco (Ninth century), and Al-Azhar University in Cairo, Egypt, (Tenth century), other countries in the region have endeavored to establish their own institutions of higher learning. The expansion of higher education in the region has been made possible largely by revenues from petroleum products (de Blij & Muller, 2007). Countries such as Saudi Arabia, Kuwait, and Bahrain all have been able to establish modern institutions of higher learning as a result of huge oil revenues.

Enrollment of students in higher education in the region is high in all the countries, especially Egypt, Israel, Saudi Arabia, Morocco, and Turkey. Some students travel to countries within the region such as Egypt, Saudi Arabia, Jordan, Turkey, or Israel to acquire higher degrees in various academic areas. Other students travel to countries outside the region for further studies. These countries include the United States of America, Great Britain, France, Australia, India, and Australia. The opportunity to study abroad or to enroll in international education programs has greatly expanded the educational opportunities for all students in the region.

REFERENCES

Ain Shams University. (2007). Statistics. http://net.shams.edu.eg/Statistics.asp.

AIU Library Newsletter. (May, 2005). Database usage statistics. *Mahammad IV Library Newsletter*, 2, 2.

Al Akhawayn University. (2005a). *Al Akhawayn University in Ifrane, 2005–2007 Catalog*. Rabat: Imprimerie el Maarif al Jadida. Available at http://www.aui.ma/DSA/academic-catalog-07-general.pdf.

———. (2005b). Database usage statistics. *Muhammad IV Library Newsletter*, 2 (May), 2.

Bahgat, G. (1999). Education in the Gulf Monarchies: Retrospect and prospect. *International Review of Education, 45*(2), 127–136.

Bahrain. Ministry of Education. (2007). Laws and Regulations. http://www.education.gov.bh/english.

Beller, M. (2001). Admission to higher education in Israel and the role of psychometric entrance test: Educational and political dilemma. *Assessment in Education*, 8(3), 315–37.

Clark, N. (2006). Education in Morocco. *World Education News & Reviews, 10*(2), 1.

de Blij, H. J., & Muller, P. O. (2007). *The world today: Concepts and regions in geography.* Atlantic Highlands, NJ: John Wiley.

Faksh, M. A. (1976). An historical survey of the educational system in Egypt. *International Review of Education, 22*(2), 234–244.

Heyworth-Dunne, J. (1938). *An introduction to the history of education in modern Egypt.* London: Luzac.

Israel Science and Technology (2008). Available at http://www.science.co.il/Univ.asp.

King Saud University. (2007). King Saud University. http://www.ksu.edu.sa.

Lulat, Y. G-M. (2005). *A history of African higher education from antiquity to the present.* Westport, CT: Praeger.

Mizikaci, F. (2006). *Higher education in Turkey.* UNESCO-CEPES Monographs on Higher Education. Bucharest, Romania: UNESCO European Center for Higher Education.

OECD (Organization for Economic Cooperation and Development). (2003). *Education Policy Analysis 2003.* Paris: OECD. Reprinted in Mizikaci (2006, p. 53).

Ouakrime, M. (2004). Country higher education profiles: Morocco. http://www.bc.edu/bc_org/avp/soe/cihe/inhea/profiles/Morocco.htm.

Saleh, M. A. (1986). Development of higher education in Saudi Arabia. *Higher Education, 15*(1/2), 17–23.

Salmi, U. M. (1999). Recent developments in Egyptian education. *World Education News & Reviews, 12*(5), 8–12.

Saudi Arabia. Ministry of Education. (2003). *The development of education.* Riyadh: Author.

Sedgwick, R. (2001). Education in Saudi Arabia. *World Education News & Reviews, 14*(6), http://www.wes.org/ewenr/01nov/practical.htm.

Sprinzak, D., Sergev, Y., Bar, E., and Leve-Mazloum, D. (1996). *Facts and figures about education in Israel.* Jerusalem. State of Israel, Ministry of Education.

Tel Aviv University, Overseas Students Program (2008). Academic information. Available from http://www.tau.ac.il/overseas/frameset.html.

UNESCO (2008). Israel: Principles and general objectives of education. http://www.ibe.unesco.org/countries/WDE/2006/Western_Europe/Israel/Israel.pdf.

University of Aleppo. (2007). University of Aleppo [in Arabic]. http://www.alepuniv.shern.net.

Chapter 6

INNOVATIONS IN THE CURRICULUM: SPECIAL NEEDS EDUCATION

Children who have learning disabilities are often socially stigmatized. They are not seen as people who are capable of learning. This situation often creates a hostile environment for such students to learn.

This attitude is not confined to students in the Middle East and North Africa. According to Gaad (2004), people in Africa and other parts of the world have similar attitudes toward children with learning disabilities. The ancient Greeks, for instance, considered the birth of twins a "disability" and therefore left them in the woods to die.

Improvements in our knowledge about human growth and development have given us a better understanding of the conditions of all children, including those with learning disabilities. The educational and scientific work of educators like Gardner and Skinner have brought into the limelight the unique nature of individuals in performing human activities such as reading, writing, and spelling. Children with learning disabilities are capable of learning but may need a longer time to master a skill that other "normal" children may learn without any difficulty. Although they may never be able to learn to be engineers or pilots, they can learn to a level that will make them useful members of society (Gaad, 2004). Again, as Gaad (2004) has pointed out: "Children with intellectual disabilities are no different from any other child when it comes to their right to have educational needs and rights.... Wherever children with intellectual disabilities are, there is an urgent need to change society's attitudes toward them" (pp. 325–26).

Scientific and psychological breakthroughs in the learning capabilities of all children have attracted the attention of curriculum planners around the world, including throughout the Middle East and North Africa (MENA) countries. In 1994, the United Nations organized a conference in Spain on the need to provide education for special needs children. At the end of the conference, a document that is now called the Salamanca Statement was issued. The statement calls for ordinary schools to include all children, irrespective of their physical, intellectual, social, emotional, linguistic, or other conditions (UNESCO, 1994). Curriculum planners in the Middle East and North Africa have therefore been reforming the education system in the region to meet the changing needs of the society. These changes are necessary because the educational planners want to make the educational system responsive to the needs of all the people in the region and the students who study in these schools.

Children going to school in the MENA region, like children in other parts of the world, have access to all kinds of educational programs to meet their individual and special needs. Although the development of special needs education is a recent innovation in the educational programs of the region, several students have benefited from its implementation and have acquired skills that were previously unimagined (Reynolds & Fletcher-Janzen, 2002). In this chapter, curriculum reform and innovative practices in the areas of special needs education will be discussed.

SPECIAL NEEDS EDUCATION

Special needs education, previously called special education, has now become part of the main curriculum standards practiced worldwide, including in the Middle East and North Africa. Special needs education falls into two main categories, one for children with learning disabilities and the other for gifted or talented students.

The term *learning disability* refers to people who learn with difficulty as a result of mental, physiological, physical, or emotional problems. There are several types of learning disabilities. Students with *autism* generally do not want to socialize with other students. They have problems communicating and interacting with others (D. D. Smith, 2001). One type of learning disability is called *dyslexia*. Students who have this disability have problem reading, spelling, or both. Some students have problems speaking or understanding the information being presented; this condition is known as *childhood aphasia*. A third type of learning disability is called *dyscalculia*. Students who have this kind of health problem find it difficult to solve mathematics problems (Zigler & Stevenson, 1993).

According to D. D. Smith (2001), "Some youngsters with learning disabilities may also display behavioral problems along with poor academic performance" (p. 130). The behavioral problem may include a child's inability to concentrate or sit for long while in the classroom. Other behavioral problems may involve fighting, biting, or excessive absence from school. Generally, children with learning disabilities:

- have difficulty reflecting over instructions and following them
- have a problem storing ideas in the brain and retrieving them when needed

- have a problem distinguishing one letter or figure from another, thus making it very difficult for them to read, spell, write, or calculate simple numbers
- have a problem with coordinated activities such as drawing, or writing. (D. D. Smith, 2001)

A second category of special needs education includes the education of children with extraordinary skills and talents. These students are often called "gifted" students. Gifted students are those "who have outstanding abilities, are capable of high performance in a specific academic area such as language arts or mathematics, or who show creativity or leadership, distinction in the visual or performing arts, or bodily talents as in gymnastics and dancing" (Rathus, 1993, p. 332). Smith, Polloway, Patton, and Dowdy (2006) see the gifted as students who "differ from their peers by having above-average intelligence and learning abilities" (p. 7). These students are generally able to cope with learning tasks without problems. Among other things, they appear to be creative, risk-taking, open to new ideas, and critical thinkers. They process or learn new ideas quickly and exhibit high task commitments (Parsons, Hinson, & Sardo-Brown, 2001).

Friend (2005) has also listed more characteristics of the gifted and talented:

Reading Behaviors

- Has early knowledge of the alphabet
- Often reads early or unlocks the reading process quickly and sometimes idiosyncratically
- Reads with expression
- Has a high interest in reading; reads voraciously

Writing Behaviors

- Displays early ability to make written sound–symbol correspondence
- Exhibits fluency and elaboration in story writing
- Uses advanced sentence structure and patterns
- May show an interest in adult topics for writing such as the state of the environment, death, war, and so on
- Writes on a topic or story for an extended period of time
- Generates may writing ideas, often of a divergent nature
- Uses precise, descriptive language to evoke an image

Speaking Behaviors

- Learns to speak early
- Has a high-receptive vocabulary
- Uses advanced sentence structure
- Uses similes, metaphors, and analogies in daily conversation
- Exhibits highly verbal behavior in speech (i.e., talks a lot, speaks rapidly, articulate well)
- Enjoys acting out story events and situations

Mathematical Behaviors

- Has early curiosity and understanding about the quantitative aspects of things
- Is able to think logically and symbolically about quantitative and spatial relationships
- Perceives and generalizes about mathematical patterns, structures, relations, and operations
- Reasons analytically, deductively, and inductively
- Abbreviates mathematical reasoning to find rational, economical solutions
- Displays flexibility and reversibility of mental process in mathematical activity
- Remembers mathematical symbols, relationships, proofs, methods of solution, and so forth
- Transfers learning to novel situations and solutions
- Displays energy and persistence in solving mathematical problems
- Has a mathematical perception of the world. (p. 583)

These characteristics are excellent because they promote mastering of new skills quickly. However, students who possess these skills often pose a different kind of problems for educators. They often finish their tasks quickly and begin to look to their teachers for extra work. If they do not get additional work, they tend to do things or engage in activities that may not be part of classroom routines. Such students may therefore require special learning tasks that offer them the challenge they need in order to benefit from the education they receive in school (Friend, 2005).

In the past, the educational system did not make provision for the education of special needs children because their condition was not seen as anything that deserved individual attention. The general argument was that children with learning disabilities were simply not fit for schoolwork. Again, the attitude of the general public toward such students was unfavorable (Mba, 1983). This was the general trend that prevailed in many of the MENA countries until the early 1940s, when the education of children became the responsibility of the central government in each country. The impetus for this recognition of special needs students came in part from external organizations such as the United Nations. UNESCO (the United Nations Educational, Scientific, and Cultural Organization) in 1948 gave worldwide recognition to the right of all children to learn in free and unfettered environments. Any education system that denied education to a section of the community was seen as a problem.

Governments worldwide accepted the challenge from UNESCO and consequently made the necessary adjustments in their educational systems. In each of the countries in the Middle East and North Africa, the government has come out with legislation providing guidelines for the education of all children, including those with learning disabilities and those who need special education because of their exceptional learning skills. Since 1948, all the countries in the region have made tremendous efforts to design educational programs that meet the needs of all students, especially those with learning disabilities.

Initially, as in the rest of the world, special needs students were not the target for curriculum planners. Students who could cope with the educational standards were always the focus of curriculum planners. These included students who had no problem with hearing, speech, or reading or writing skills. On the other hand, students who had learning disabilities or special talents were not taken into consideration when curriculum standards were planned or designed.

The education of the gifted does not pose as big a challenge for curriculum planners as that for students with learning disabilities. This implies that the focus of the provision of special needs education is often on meeting the needs of students with learning disabilities rather than those with special gifts and talents. Thus, when people talk about special needs education, they often mean education for those with learning disabilities such as children with hearing, reading, writing, speaking, or vision problems.

In all the MENA countries, curriculum planners have now made the education of special needs students part of the educational system. Countries such as Bahrain, Egypt, Israel, Jordan, Kuwait, Lebanon, Libya, Saudi Arabia, the United Arab Emirates, Qatar, and Yemen have all made significant progress in providing special needs education for students who require individualized services in learning. Often governments in the region and nongovernmental organizations (NGOs) such as the World Bank and the United Nations team up to provide excellent learning environments for children who need special tools in learning. Great Britain, the United States, France, and Japan are some of the foreign countries that have made significant contributions toward the development of special needs education for students in the region.

THE ENVIRONMENT FOR SPECIAL NEEDS STUDENTS

The appropriate place for the education of special needs students has always been a problem for educators. Some people strongly believe that all students, irrespective of their condition, should be educated in the same or similar environments (Ainscow, 1997). They argue that any arrangement short of this is equal to discrimination. Other educators believe that the appropriate place for the education of the special needs student is a self-contained environment where such students can learn at their own rate without exerting undue pressure on teachers and students who may happen to be in the same learning environment as the special needs students.

In the Middle East and North Africa, special needs students often attend the same school as regular students. The idea behind this approach is to offer all students equal opportunity to learn in the same environment. Again, this model, it is argued, provides all students the opportunity to interact and to get a better understanding of the learning needs of each group. In some cases, especially where the condition of the special needs students becomes a distraction for their classmates, such students are educated in different classrooms. Other students with learning disabilities are, however, permitted to study in the same classroom with the regular students, but are offered certain courses in pulled-out environments. Such arrangements help special needs students learn at their own rate and thus make the most of their time spent in the classroom (Alghazo & Naggar, 2004; Al-Shammari & Yawkey, 2007; Scott & Shearer-Lingo, 2002).

Inclusion is a concept that is often not clearly understood by the public. According to Friend (2005), "Inclusion is a belief system shared by every member of a school as a learning community—teachers, administrators, other staff members, students, and parents—about the responsibility of educating all students so that they can reach their potential" (p. 22). Friend argues further that "inclusion is not about where students sit as much as it is about how adults and classmates welcome all students to access learning and recognize that the diversity of learners in today's schools dictates that no single approach is appropriate for all" (p. 22).

According to UNESCO (2005), inclusion is nothing more than

a process of addressing and responding to the diversity of needs of all learners through increasing participation in learning, cultures and communities, and reducing exclusion within and from education. It involves changes and modifications in content, approaches, structures and strategies, with a common vision which covers all children of the appropriate age range and a conviction that it is the responsibility of the regular system to educate all children. (p. 13)

UNESCO goes on to make it clear what may or may not constitute inclusive education, as shown in figure 6.1.

According to UNESCO, inclusion is a concept that has gradually evolved into the curriculum over the years. The right of all children to a proper education was recognized by the United Nations in 1948, three years after World War II. Since then, the attention of the world has focused on the educational needs of all children, irrespective of their social, physical, emotional, ethnic, or racial background.

Inclusive education implies that gifted students and students with learning disabilities, as well as those who work at the normal rate at school, learn together. As Friend (2005) has pointed out, inclusive education "is a belief system that can only be implemented when all staff understand and adopt it" (p. 22). Friend adds that, to some people, "the only way that a school can truly demonstrate an inclusive belief system is to ensure that *all* students fully participate in general education. Without this approach, … some students will be excluded forever because they cannot meet the traditional academic standards of that setting" (p. 22).

UNESCO (2005, p. 24) describes the gradual development and understanding of inclusive education by the steps of denial, acceptance (benevolence, charity), understanding, and finally knowledge. It shows that knowledge about the condition of students with special learning needs is the key to the acceptance and practice of inclusive education.

Figure 6.1
What Inclusive Education Implies and What It Does Not

Inclusion IS about:	Inclusion is NOT about:
☺ welcoming diversity	☹ reforms of special education alone, but reform of both the formal and non-formal education system
☺ benefiting all learners, not only targeting the excluded	☹ responding only to diversity, but also improving the quality of education for all learners
☺ children in school who may feel excluded	☹ special schools but perhaps additional support to students within the regular school system
☺ providing equal access to education or making certain provisions for certain categories of children without excluding them	☹ meeting the needs of children with disabilities only
	☹ meeting one child's needs at the expense of another child

Source: UNESCO (2005, p. 15).

To lend empirical support to the argument for inclusion, UNESCO (1999) conducted research in some selected countries and concluded that students with learning disabilities make significant progress when they learn in a nonisolated, nonthreatening environment. It reported a study of the inclusion of a student with a disability in the regular school environment in Palestine, concluding that the student was able to make friends and interact with the other students, and eventually these developments boosted the academic achievement of the student who had the learning disability.

CATEGORIES OF SPECIAL NEEDS STUDENTS

Special needs students are generally categorized into several groups: mental retardation/severe learning difficulties, visual impairment, hearing impairment, emotional and behavioral disturbance, physical or motor disabilities, and language disorder. Students within each category of disability receive a special kind of education that meets their condition. This may take place in a special education class, a resource room, special classes in regular schools, or a boarding school set up for special needs students.

FUNDING FOR SPECIAL NEEDS EDUCATION

Special needs education in the Middle East and North Africa is generally the responsibility of each national government. Most of the funding therefore comes from the governments. Other sources include voluntary organizations and parents. For instance, in the 1994/1995 school year, the United Arab Emirates government covered 70 percent of the cost of providing appropriate education for special needs students; voluntary organizations added 20 percent; and parents; 10 percent.

TEACHER PREPARATION

Teachers who work in special needs institutions need particular training to handle the students under their care (Angelides, Stylianou, & Gibbs, 2006). To this end, all the countries in the Middle East and North Africa have set up programs in their teacher training institutions to equip special education teachers with the skills they will need in handling the education and training of special needs students. Until the development of these local teacher training institutions, most of the teachers working in special needs institutions received their training in Egypt or abroad, especially in the United States, Britain, or France (Gerner, 1985). However, many of the teachers were simply recruited from experienced teachers and had no special training to deal with the needs of special needs students.

Today, as a result of the greater attention governments in the region have given to the education of special needs students, most of the MENA countries have their own educational institutions that prepare special needs teachers. Some experienced teachers do not have to go back to school to be certified to teach special education classes; they attend in-service training or workshops for a number of months and then become qualified to teach special needs classes. Other teachers attend four-year teacher preparation courses to be certified to teach special education courses.

Some of the universities and colleges in the region that prepare special needs education teachers are:

- Ain Shams University, Cairo
- Cairo University, Cairo
- Al-Hussein Bin Talal University, Jordan
- United Arab Emirates University, Al Ain, United Arab Emirates
- Bahrain University College, Bahrain
- King Abdul Aziz (Education), Jeddah, Saudi Arabia
- Kuwait University, Kuwait City, Kuwait
- Qatar University (Education), Qatar
- Riyadh University, Riyadh, Saudi Arabia
- American University of Beirut, Beirut, Lebanon
- Lebanese American University, Beirut and Byblos, Lebanon
- Anadolu University, Eskisehir, Turkey
- Tel-Hai Academic College, Tel Hai, Israel
- Oranim College, Oranim, Israel
- David Yellin College of Education, Jerusalem
- Talpiot College, Tel Aviv, Israel

- Tel Aviv University, Tel Aviv, Israel
- Gordon College, Haifa, Israel

Some prospective special needs teachers study for a period of four years for their bachelor's degree. Others complete two-year diploma courses to augment their previous academic credentials to qualify them to teach special needs students. The courses the teachers take include human development, pedagogy, psychology of human learning, and assessment. For instance, table 6.1 lists the course of study that special education teachers take in Turkey to qualify as teachers of special needs students. This is a sample program that teachers of special needs students complete at the university or at teacher training colleges. Each country adapts the programs to meet local needs. However, the core content remains the same.

Technology now plays a major role in the education of special needs students. Consequently, educational technology forms part of the education of these teachers as well. Software programs the teachers learn to use include word processing, presentation programs such as Microsoft PowerPoint, and oral reading software. Other technological tools include assistive listening devices such as hearing aids, other devices that help these students improve their communication skills, and equipment designed for the low-vision students such as magnifiers, closed-circuit television, and monoculars (T. E. C. Smith et al., 2006).

THE ROLE OF GOVERNMENT

After independence, each government in the region assumed responsibility for the education of all children. Each country saw education as a human right and therefore made every effort to extend education to all children, irrespective of their physical, emotional, physiological, or mental condition.

Legislation was introduced that made the state responsible for the education of all children. For instance, the 1962 Kuwaiti National Constitution has certain clauses that clearly spell out the role of the government in the provision of education for all children, including those with special needs. Article 10 states, "The State shall care for the young and shall protect them from abuse as well as from moral, physical and spiritual neglect." Article 13 says, "Education is a basic component to be provided and supervised by the State." And Article 40 adds: "Education is a right for all citizens to be provided by the State in accordance with the law and in keeping with the general system and ethics. Education is compulsory and free of charge in its primary stages, according to the law."

According to Law No. 1 of 1965, education is compulsory and free of charge for all Kuwaiti children from the first grade of primary education (age 6) to the end of the intermediate or preparatory level. This law makes it incumbent on the state to provide school premises, books, teachers, and all that is necessary in terms of human and material means to guarantee the success of compulsory education.

Table 6.1
Program in Education of the Mentally Disabled

First Semester
Fundamentals of Information Technology
Introduction to Teacher Training
Health Science and First Aid
Ataturk's Principles and History of Turkish Revolution I
Turkish I: Writing Skills
Special Education

Second Semester
Music
Educational Research and Report Writing
Ataturk's Principles and History of Turkish Revolution II
Turkish II: Speaking Skills
Introduction: Mentally Handicapped Children
Changing Attitudes toward the Handicapped
Individual Differences and Psychological Approaches
Foreign Language Courses

Third Semester
Human Development and Learning
Developing Individualized Education Programs and Evaluation
Education of the Mentally Handicapped
Language Development and Communication
Educational and Behavioral Assessment
Integration and Special Education Support Services
Elective Courses

Fourth Semester
Teaching Music to the Mentally Handicapped
Early Childhood Education for the Mentally Handicapped
Teaching Communication Skills to the Mentally Handicapped
Teaching Concepts and Skills to the Mentally Handicapped
Behavior Management
Elective Courses

Fifth Semester
Use of Technology and Materials Development
Teaching Reading and Writing to the Mentally Handicapped
Teaching Science to the Mentally Handicapped
Teaching Mathematics to the Mentally Handicapped
Preparing Integration Programs
Elective Courses

Sixth Semester
Classroom Management
Teaching Turkish to the Mentally Handicapped
Teaching Social Sciences and Social Studies to the Mentally Handicapped
Teaching Games and Physical Education to the Mentally Handicapped

Teaching Art to the Mentally Handicapped
Teaching Self-Care Skills to the Mentally Handicapped

Seventh Semester
Teaching Experience I (Field Base Experiences)
Preparing and Implementing Assessment Tools for Students with Mental Retardation
Developing Measurement Materials to Determine the Performance Level
Training and Guiding Parents of Mentally Handicapped Children

Eighth Semester
Practicum Teaching Experience II (Field Base Experiences)
Developing Lesson Plans for the Trainable Mentally Handicapped
Developing Instructional Materials for the Mentally Handicapped
School Programming and Education Settings for Mentally Handicapped Children
Placing and Monitoring Trainable Mentally Handicapped Children

Source: Cavkaytar (2006, p. 43).

The Israeli government in 1988 passed the Special Education Law, which states that

the purpose of special education is to advance and develop the abilities and potential of handicapped children, to correct and improve their physical, mental, psychological and behavioural performance, to convey knowledge, skills, and habits and to adapt them to behaviour acceptable to society with the purpose of becoming part of it and being integrated in the world of work.

The law provides for special education for individuals between the ages of 3 and 21 whose capacity for adaptive behaviour is limited and who are in need of such education, including physiotherapy, speech therapy, and occupational therapy, as well as treatment in additional areas. (Israel, 1996, p. 4)

In Turkey, special education is provided by the government under Special Education Law 573. The main provisions of the law are as follows:

(a) All the individuals who are in need of special education will benefit from the special education services in line with their interests, wishes, adequacies and abilities.
(b) Education of the individuals who are in need of special education will start at an early age.
(c) The special education services will be planned and provided without separating the individuals who are in need of special education from their social and physical environments as much as possible.
(d) It will be a priority to educate those individuals who are in need of special education together with other individuals by taking those individuals' educational performances into consideration and by making adaptations in the aim, content and teaching processes.
(e) Cooperation will be established with the institutions and organizations that provide all types of rehabilitation for the education of individuals who are in need of special education to continue their education at all levels and with all types uninterruptedly.

(f) Individualized education plans will be developed for the individuals who are in need of special education and the educational programs will be implemented as individualized.

(g) Opinions of the organizations working for the individuals who are in need of special education will be asked for the development of special education policies.

(h) The special education services will be planned so as to cover the social interaction and mutual adaptation process of the individuals who are in need of special education. (Cavkaytar, 2006, p. 41)

The general idea is that by introducing national laws to provide special needs education for all the children in the region, all students irrespective of their physical abilities will have the opportunity to receive formal education. In many cases, special needs students enroll in the same school as "regular" students. Students with severe mental or physical problems, however, get their instruction in pull-out programs. These laws have helped parents find appropriate avenues to educate their children with learning disabilities.

Special education schools and facilities are provided from a number of sources. Throughout the region, government and the private sector have collaborated to establish educational facilities for students with learning disabilities. In this case, the efforts of the governments are complemented with extra funds and resources. The United Nations, the World Bank, and UNICEF are some of the agencies that help promote special needs education in the region.

SPECIAL NEEDS EDUCATION IN EGYPT

Egypt has for several decades paid attention to the education of special needs students. These may be students with a learning disability or those who need special learning facilities in order to cope with regular schoolwork. Special education classes broadly categorized as visual, auditory, and mental have been set up in the country to help develop the potential labor skills of these students. These three categories of special needs education often constitute the core special education programs.

The goals of special needs education in Egypt as laid out in a government report are as follows:

- To establish specialized schools for educating children with special needs
- To prepare qualified teachers who are able to meet the demands of special needs students
- To provide assistive technologies that meet the teaching and learning styles of special needs students
- To prepare curricula and textbooks that are suitable for teaching special needs students. (Egypt, 2004)

Gifted and talented students also receive attention from the government in designing appropriate education to meet their special needs. These students are identified very early in the education process and given help to develop to their full potential (Elmenoufy, 2007).

All developed schools for special needs students have computer laboratories where teachers use modern technology or assistive technology to help students master basic or key concepts in the curriculum. Some special needs schools have been linked to the Internet to help teachers utilize the vast resources on the Internet in their teaching.

Since 1993, the number of students enrolled in special education classes has continued to soar. In 1993, the number of special education schools was 67, with 797 students enrolled and a total of 1,386 teachers working in these schools. In one year, the number of schools increased to 96 with a total enrollment of 813 and 1,495 teachers employed. By the close of the 1995 academic year, the number of schools offering special education classes rose to 107 with an enrollment of 8,169 and 1,747 teachers (see table 6.2).

As compared to the other sectors of the educational system in Egypt, educational facilities for special needs students have been increasing over the last decade. Table 6.3 illustrates comparative increases in the enrollment patterns of students in Egypt. From the table, it is clear that enrollments for special needs students had the second highest increase ratio between 1991 and 2000. The greatest increase was in one-classroom schools, a new education system that offers education to students in remote parts of the country, especially rural students who had previously dropped out of school. One-classroom schools often offer opportunities for disadvantaged students, especially young girls, to acquire basic education skills.

SPECIAL NEEDS EDUCATION IN ISRAEL

According to the JDC-Brookdale Institute (2004), Israel in 2003 had approximately 177,000 children (7.7% of all children) who suffered from disabilities of various kinds. These included

deafness, paralysis, retardation, learning disabilities and severe behavior problems, cancer or other chronic diseases requiring medical or para-medical care on a regular basis. Of them, there are some 93,000 (4.0% of all children) whose main disability is a learning or behavioral disability. (p. 2)

To meet the challenge of educating all children in Israel, the government has developed an extensive education system for special needs students. Like the other countries in the region, the Israeli government is responsible for the education of all children in the country. The Ministry of Education is responsible for all aspects of special needs education. However, other ministries also participate in the provision of education for special needs students. For instance, the Ministry of Health is responsible for screening infants for any signs of disability. The Ministry of Labor and Social Welfare is responsible for meeting the needs of children with mental retardation (UNESCO, 1995).

Table 6.2
Growth in Special Education in Egypt, 1993–1995

Handicap	Number of schools			Number of classes			Number of pupils			Number of teachers		
	1993	1994	1995	1993	1994	1995	1993	1994	1995	1993	1994	1995
Visual	19	21	25	187	205	224	1,866	2,135	2,159	471	492	588
Auditory	40	57	95	622	676	756	6,762	7,024	8,496	1,174	1,395	1,432
Mental	67	96	107	767	813	786	6,945	7,535	8,169	1,386	1,495	1,747

Source: International Bureau of Education (2008). http://www.ibe.unesco.org/countries/WDE/2006/ARAB_STATES/Egypt/Egypt.pdf.

Table 6.3
Access to Education in Egypt, 1991–2000

Stage	1991/92	1999/2000	Increase	Increase Ratio
Kindergarten	223,051	354,435	131,384	58.90%
Primary	6,541,725	7,224,989	689,264	10.44%
Preparatory	3,593,365	4,345,356	751,991	20.92%
General Secondary	572,026	1,039,958	467,930	81.80%
Technical Secondary	1,110,184	1,913,022	802,838	72.32%
Special Education	14,428	29,396	14,968	103.7%
One-Classroom Schools	3,165	51,461	48,296	1,525.9%

Source: Egypt, National Center for Educational Research and Development (2001, p. 16).

The goals of special needs education in Israel are:

• To advance and develop the potential skills and abilities of the special needs child
• To correct and enhance the physical, mental, emotional and behavioral functioning
• To impart to the special needs student knowledge, skills, and habits
• To help the special needs children learn acceptable social behavior with the goal of facilitating their integration into society and employment

These are the main objectives that drive government efforts in designing special education programs in the country. The goals are based on the Special Education Law of 1988, which guarantees the right of all children to education in an appropriate environment (International Bureau of Education, 2008).

The Israeli government has set up a Special Needs Committee that works with schools to find placements for special needs students. Once identified, the students are then enrolled in educational institutions that have facilities to help the students learn under appropriate circumstances. Many of the special needs students are enrolled in regular schools as part of the inclusive education process.

In Israel, several categories of students with special needs are defined and identified. These include:

• Mental retardation/severe learning difficulties
• Emotional and behavioral disorders
• Physical/motor disabilities
• Visual impairment
• Language disorders
• Chronic illness
• Learning disabilities
• Hearing impairment

- Multiple and severe handicaps
- Deafness
- Cerebral palsy
- Autism (UNESCO, 1995; Meadan & Gumpel, 2002)

The development of *mainstreaming* in Israel has led to a reduction in the number of students classified as having special needs. As seen in figure 6.2, the percentage of students in special education programs as compared with the general student body has decreased from 3.5% in the 1989/1990 school year to 2.3% in 2002/2003. The numbers in parentheses in the figure represent the number of students in special education models (students in special education schools as well as students in special classes located in regular schools) (International Bureau of Education, 2008).

Nonprofit organizations also participate in the education of students with special needs. These include the Nitzan Association, which was founded in

Figure 6.2
Pupils in Special Education (Hebrew Education and Arab Education)

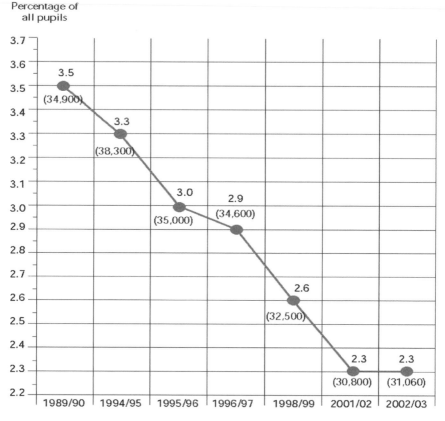

Source: Israel, Ministry of Education, Culture, and Sport (2004, p. 72).

1964 by a group of parents who saw the need to team up to find a better way of educating their children with learning disabilities (Danino, 2006). Other voluntary associations include:

- AHADA (parent organization of the United Kibbutz Movement on behalf of kibbutz children with special needs)
- AKIM (national organization for persons with mental retardation)
- ALOOT (national organization for autistic children)
- Bezkhoot (legal advocacy organization established by the civil liberties organization Aguda LeZechooyot HaEzrach)
- Center for Epilepsy (national center in Haifa providing information and counseling)
- Central Library for Persons with Blindness and Visual Impairments
- Council for the Welfare of the Child (advocacy organization focusing on problems of child abuse and neglect)
- ELI (child advocacy organization)
- ELKAN (organization working on behalf of troubled youth)
- EYAL (national organization for epilepsy)
- GAN HARMONY (organization advocating inclusion of children with special needs in regular educational settings)
- HILA (national advocacy organization for parents of children in special education)
- ILAN (national organization for children with physical disabilities)
- JOINT Israel (Israel office of the Joint Distribution Committee, an international Jewish organization, which initiates, sponsors, and funds many projects in Israel on behalf of people with special needs)
- MICHA (national organization serving preschool children with deafness and hearing impairments)
- MILBAT (national information center on adaptive equipment, transportation, and construction for people with disabilities)
- No'ar HaDemama (national organization for hearing-impaired youth)
- Ozen Kashevet Leyeladim Veno'ar (organization providing counseling for children in crisis and their families)
- SHEMA (national organization for persons with hearing impairments)
- Tikva (national organization on behalf of persons with brain injury)
- Yad Sara (national organization lending adaptive medical equipment)
- YATED (national organization on behalf of persons with Down Syndrome and their families)

As part of the mainstreaming process, students whose disabilities are relatively mild are encouraged to study in the regular classrooms "if they are treated with tolerance, if others are aware of their particular type of problem, and if the school system can develop special programs for them with the regular classroom framework" (Israel, 1996, p. 7).

Special education classes are offered from preschool through high school. There are categorical programs in regular schools for special needs students. These special classes in regular schools can be divided into three major groups:

- Classes for children with learning disabilities
- Classes for children with hearing impairments

- Generic special classes for a variety of mild emotional, behavioral, cognitive and/or mental handicaps

Children are placed in these special programs in the regular schools by the Placement Committee, as mandated by the Special Education Law passed by the Knesset in 1988 (Goldgraber, 1997).

Another avenue for educating children with special needs in Israel is through special educational programs in special schools. Most of these schools are located in the urban areas. Schools that provide these programs include:

- Generic special education schools. These are the traditional special schools serving a variety of children with mild mental, emotional, behavioral and learning handicaps
- Schools for children with physically impairments
- Schools for children with hearing impairments
- Schools for children with mild and moderate mental retardation
- Schools for children with moderate, severe, and profound mental retardation
- Schools for children with autism, psychoses, or schizophrenia
- Schools for children with severe emotional, behavioral, and/or adjustment problems
- Vocational post-elementary schools (Miftanim) serving children with learning, behavioral, and adjustment difficulties
- Schools for children with blindness. (Goldgraber, 1997)

Special Needs Students in the Regular Classrooms

Special education teachers play a significant role in the education of students with special needs. These teachers have been specially trained to teach children with special needs. In the classroom, they give all students the same content. Depending upon the level or severity of the condition of the special needs student in the regular classroom, teachers are assisted by intervention specialists, who often isolate the special needs student and work with him or her at a different pace, using different instructional methods and tools.

The resource room in the regular schools serves as "integration support service" for special needs students. In the resource rooms, students receive remedial instruction. The resource rooms become very important, especially when the students need special tools to learn. Here, teachers pay attention to the special conditions of the children as they teach them. In many cases, the children are not "pushed." They learn at their own rate and take breaks as necessary.

Gifted Students in Israel

Gifted students in Israel are not left out of the government efforts to provide appropriate education for all children. As in other countries in the MENA region, the education of gifted and talented students does not attract the attention of the government and the public like that of students with learning disabilities. Nevertheless, the Israeli government considers the education of gifted and talented students very important in order "to utilize the human potential that giftedness implies for the sake of the country and society" (Peyser, 2005, p. 230).

The Ministry of Education in Israel has set up a separate department to identify and provide appropriate education for gifted students. The process of selection is tedious and cumbersome. A national test is conducted every year in grades 2 and 3 to select these students. The selection process is conducted in two stages.

Once the students are screened through achievement tests, they are placed in different programs based upon their individual ability. Those who perform well are placed in one of three programs: special classes, pull-out weekly enrichment classes, and afternoon extracurricular activities classes.

SPECIAL NEEDS EDUCATION IN BAHRAIN

In 1986, the government of Bahrain introduced an educational law that led to the recognition of the educational needs of students with learning disabilities. These included slow learners and the physically handicapped, blind, deaf, and mentally retarded. At the same time, the special needs of gifted students were also recognized. The government established a Special Education Unit within the Directorate of Student Activities and Services. The main responsibility of this unit is the identification of children with special needs for training in public schools.

The main impetus for the establishment of special needs educational programs in Bahrain emanated from a recommendation made by UNESCO in 1988/1989. Following this recommendation, the government set up a pilot program to study the possibility of reforming the school curriculum to cater for the needs of all students. It started with eight primary schools, seven for boys and one for girls.

The main objective for the establishment of special needs education in Bahrain is the desire of the government to design appropriate education for all children. Like the other countries in the region, the government is solely responsible for the education of special needs students. The government, through the Ministry of Education and the Ministry of Social Affairs, lays the groundwork for the education of special needs students.

Bahrain has an elaborate program for special needs education. In 1992, the government moved a step further and integrated special needs students into regular schools. Students with mild learning disabilities such as Down syndrome are integrated into the regular classrooms so as to provide them with a natural learning environment, according to Ministerial Decision 189/2001, dated October 13, 2001. Specially trained and certified teachers teach these students and are assisted by intervention specialists.

To help students with a learning disability to learn at their own rate, students with special needs are taught in resource rooms so they will not distract the other students from learning. Students with severe learning disabilities, however, are taught in special schools designed to meet their conditions. For instance, blind students can learn in specially designed learning centers until they reach a secondary stage in special government educational institutions.

As in the other countries in the MENA region, nonprofit organizations also participate in the development, organization, and administration of education for special needs students. These organizations and institutions include the Al-Amal Institute, Social Rehabilitation Center, Rehabilitation Institute for Autism Patients and Related Diseases (RIA), Alia Communication Difficulties Center, Bahrain Center for Care and Rehabilitation for Persons with Special Needs, Hope Institute for Handicapped Children, Blind Friendship Kindergarten, Al Rama Center, Al Rashad Center, and National Disabled Services Establishment.

THE SAUDI-BAHRAIN INSTITUTE FOR THE BLIND

The Saudi-Bahrain Institute for the Blind is a regional educational facility for the visually impaired that uses the curriculum established by the government of Bahrain to educate special needs children. It is a joint project between the governments of Saudi Arabia and Bahrain and is coeducational. The institute provides academic and health training for all enrolled students. Those who successfully complete their intermediate-level education are transferred to regular secondary schools to continue their education. The institute uses Braille as a method of instruction.

The objectives of the Saudi-Bahrain Institute for the Blind include:

1. Teaching blind people and preparing them for higher studies
2. Qualifying blind people for work
3. Taking care of and giving guidance to the blind
4. Highlighting the blind's role in society through their participation in various activities locally and abroad
5. Displaying the blind's products by holding fairs and exhibitions
6. Training the blind physically in order to make them acquire physical fitness and giving them the opportunity to participate in competitions and physical exercises, both locally and abroad
7. Encouraging the blind to read, enabling them to acquire knowledge by benefiting from published copied books available in the institute's library
8. Training the blind to move freely and understand directions by using a cane

To earn admission to this institute, a student must be blind or of very weak sight, without having any other disability, and needs to submit a medical certificate from the Ministry of Health proving this condition. Participants in the academic stage can be between ages 6 and 20. The academic section consists of three stages:

- Nurseries for the blind, lasting two or three years, according to the age of the participants
- Primary stage, lasting six years
- Intermediate stage, lasting three years

Class programs include educational and training activities. The institute provides students with the equipment, advanced educational aids, and Braille-published textbooks. Out-of-class programs and activities include social and cultural events such as trips, seminars, lectures, cultural competitions, and functions. Sports activities include participation in local competitions with clubs and schools for other students. There are also activities abroad and miscellaneous training courses for the institute's teachers and advisors from time to time in order to improve their skills and acquaint them with advancements in the field. Finally, there is follow-up on the life of students after they graduate to help them find proper jobs and to ensure that they are adapting in their society and leading a stable and normal life (Bahrain, Ministry of Education, 2008).

The Social Rehabilitation Center

The Social Rehabilitation Center, organized by the Ministry of Labor and Social Affairs, consists of four units:

- Hearing Defect Unit, for 3- to 10-year-old children. The curriculum includes reading, speech training, writing, sign language, and finger alphabet.
- Special Education Unit, for children ages 12 to 15. The curriculum includes vocational as well as academic programs.
- Vocational Rehabilitation Unit, for students ages 16 years old and over.
- Craft Workshop Unit for 16-year-olds. Training programs focus on trades like carpentry, farming, tailoring, home economics, special skills, and handicrafts. (Bahrain Ministry of Education, 2008)

The Role of Nongovernmental Organizations

NGOs also play a major role in offering special needs education and facilities for students in the region. In Lebanon, Mounira Solh established the first educational institute for the mentally handicapped in the country in 1959 to meet the rising needs of children who were mentally challenged in performing everyday tasks. The institute organizes academic and social activities for the students enrolled there.

In Bahrain, the Al-Amal Institute offers special education programs to the mentally retarded. This institute was established by the Child and Motherhood Care Society. Students admitted to the institute must meet a few conditions: They must not have any other disabilities that may impair their education while in the institute, and they must be between 6 and 12 years old for educational programs and between 12 and 15 years old for vocational programs. The institute designs individual educational programs (IEPs) for the students. This is specially done to provide appropriate and individualized education for each student.

In Qatar, the Qatar Association for the Special Needs was established in 1992 to help provide special education for needy children. This association has three branches throughout the country: the Cultural and Social Center, the Educational Center, and Mother's Awareness Center. This nongovernmental association aims to provide education and resources for meeting basic needs in life to children with various disabilities. It produces and imports educational aids and artificial limbs for deserving students.

For the 2004/2005 school year, the private sector made a significant contribution toward the education of special needs in Qatar. For this year, 65 percent of the schools under the Ministry of Education provided accommodation for special needs students; at the same time 90 percent of the schools under private management provided learning facilities for students with learning disabilities. Fifty-six percent of the independent schools, that is, schools funded by the government but autonomous in the organization and administration of the school, also had facilities for students with learning disabilities (Qatar, 2006).

SUMMARY

The Middle East and North Africa region has made significant progress in providing suitable education for all students who need special education. There are two main categories of special needs students. One group is made up of students who are so talented that instruction in the normal classroom does not meet their learning needs. These students are often described as "gifted and talented." These students require a fast-paced and challenging curriculum. Such learning environments are not found in the ordinary classrooms, and hence governments in the region have set up different educational programs for such students.

The other category of special needs students are those with learning disabilities. These form the bulk of special needs educational programs because they tend to be numerous. Governments in the region have teamed with NGOs to provide appropriate education for all students with special needs. Although special needs education is a relatively new program in the region, most of the students who require special education are able to get the education they require to equip them with basic skills.

REFERENCES

Ainscow, M. (1997). Towards inclusive schooling. *British Journal of Special Education,* *24*(1), 3–6.

Alghazo, E. M., & Naggar, E. E. (2004). General education teachers in the United Arab Emirates and their acceptance of the inclusion of students with disabilities. *British Journal of Special Education, 31*(2), 94–99.

Al-Shammari, Z., & Yawkey, T. D. (2007). Examining the development and recommen-
    dations for special education in the state of Kuwait: An evolving program. *Education,*
    127(4), 534–40.
Angelides, P. A., Stylianou, T., & Gibbs, P. (2006). Preparing teachers for inclusive edu-
    cation in Cyprus. *Teaching and Teacher Education, 22,* 513–22.
Bahrain. Ministry of Education. (2008). *Education.* http://www.education.gov.bh/eng-
    lish/educational-statistics/index.asp.
———. (2008). The Saudi-Bahrain Institute for the Blind. Retrieved from http://
    www.blindinstitute.org/english/page-6.htm.
Cavkaytar, A. (2006). Teacher training on special education in Turkey. *Turkish Online*
    Journal of Educational Technology, 5(3), Article 7, http://www.tojet.net/volumes/
    v5i3.pdf.
Danino, M. (2006). In the absence of a law to protect their rights, Israeli students with
    learning disabilities fall between the cracks. Paper presented at the Learning Disabil-
    ities Association of America national conference, Jacksonville, Florida, March. Avail-
    able at http://eng.nitzan-israel.org.il/learning_disabilities_in_israel_nitzan_ld.
Egypt. (2004). *Development of education in Arab Republic of Egypt, 2000–2004.* Cairo:
    Author.
Egypt. National Center for Educational Research and Development. (2001). *Education*
    development: National report of Arab Republic of Egypt from 1990–2000. Cairo:
    Author.
Elmenoufy, S. G. (2007). Mathematics education for the gifted in Egypt. *Proceedings of*
    the British Society for Research into Learning Mathematics, 27(2). Available at http://
    www.bsrlm.org.uk/IPs/ip27-2/BSRLM-IP-27-2-03.pdf.
Friend, M. (2005). *Special education: Contemporary perspectives for school professionals.*
    Boston: Pearson.
Gaad, E. (2004). Cross-cultural perspectives on the effect of cultural attitudes towards
    inclusion for children with intellectual disabilities. *Journal of Inclusive Education,*
    8(3), 311–328.
Gerner, M. (1985). The school psychologist in Saudi Arabia. *School Psychology Interna-*
    tional, 6, 88–94.
Goldgraber, Y. (1997). Special education in Israel. http://www.kinneret.co.il/benzev/
    yacov/spedartc.htm.
International Bureau of Education (2008). *World data on education* (web edition).
    http://www.ibe.unesco.org.
Israel. (1996). Israel: National report, 1996. Report presented to the 45th session of the
    International Conference on Education, Geneva, September 30–October 5. Available
    at http://www.ibe.unesco.org/countries/countryDossier/natrep96/israel96.pdf.
Israel. Ministry of Education, Culture, and Sport. (2004). *Facts and figures.* Jerusalem:
    Author.
JDC-Brookdale Institute. (2004). *People with disability in Israel: Facts and figures.* Dis-
    ability Research Unit, JDC-Israel, Unit for Disabilities and Rehabilitation.
Mba, P. O. (1983). Trends in education of the handicapped children in developing
    countries with particular reference to Africa. *B.C. Journal of Special Education, 7*(3),
    273–78.
Meadan, H., & Gumpel, T. P. (2002). Special education in Israel. *Council for Excep-*
    tional Children, 34(5), 16–20.

Parsons, R. D., Hinson, S. L., & Sardo-Brown, D. (2001). *Educational psychology: A practitioner-researcher model of teaching.* Belmont, CA: Wadsworth.

Peyser, M. (2005). Identifying and nurturing gifted children in Israel. *International Journal for the Advancement of Counseling, 27*(2), 229–43.

Qatar. Supreme Education Council. Evaluation Institute. (2006). *Schools and schooling in Qatar, 2004–2006.* Available at http://www.english.education.gov.qa.

Rathus, S. A. (1993). *Psychology* (5th ed.). Fort Worth, TX: Harcourt Brace Jovanovich College Publishers.

Reynolds, C. R., & Fletcher-Janzen, E. (2002). *Concise encyclopedia of special education.* New York: John Wiley & Sons.

Scott, T. M., & Shearer-Lingo, A. (2002). The effects of reading fluency instruction on the academic and behavioral success of middle school students in a self-contained EBD classroom. *Preventing School Failure, 46*(4), 167–73.

Smith, D. D. (2001). *Introduction to special education: Teaching in an age of opportunity* (4th ed.). Boston: Allyn & Bacon.

Smith, T. E. C., Polloway, E. A., Patton, J. R., & Dowdy, C. A. (2006). *Teaching students with special needs in inclusive settings.* Boston: Allyn & Bacon.

UNESCO. (1994). *The Salamanca Statement and framework for action on special needs Education.* Paris: Author.

———. (1995). *Review of the present situation in special needs education.* Paris: Author.

———. (1999). *Students with disabilities in regular schools.* Paris: Author.

———. (2005). *Guidelines for inclusion: Ensuring access to education for all.* Paris: Author.

Zigler, E. F., & Stevenson, M. F. (1993). *Children in a changing world: Development and social issues.* Pacific Grove, CA: Brooks/Cole.

Chapter 7

GENDER AND SCHOOLING

Differential education for males and females has a long history in the Middle East and North Africa. Traditionally, many parents did not see the need to send their daughters to school because the traditional role women played did not require any formal schooling (Heyworth-Dunne, 1938). The traditional role of women in the region, as in other parts of the globe, included cooking, childbearing, caring for children, working on the farm, or being at home to complete many household chores such as cleaning the house. In other words, girls were expected to stay home and be responsible for providing food for the entire family. The skills for successfully completing these tasks were easily acquired from mothers at home.

Boys, on the other hand, were expected to be breadwinners. They were expected to leave the home to look for resources that could help feed, clothe, and keep the family in a safe and secure environment. These were skills that the father alone could not help the young boy acquire, and so there was a need for the young boy to leave home and join other male members in the community to learn the art of caring for or providing for a family.

The World Bank (2004) sums up the gender-role elements as follows:

- The centrality of the family, rather than the individual, is the main unit of society, in which men and women play complementary not equal roles. Both men and women view the family as a cultural asset.
- Recognition of the man as the sole breadwinner of the family.
- A code of modesty that rests family honor and dignity on the reputation of the woman, with restrictions on interactions between men and women.
- An unequal balance of power in the private sphere that is anchored in family laws.

This paradigm presumes that women will marry (early), that their most important contribution to the family and society will be as homemaker and mother, that households will be headed by men who have jobs that allow them to provide for their families, that women will depend on men for support, and that the man's responsibility for supporting his wife and family justifies his control over his wife's interactions in the public sphere. (p. 10)

This approach has indeed raised the illiteracy rate of females and restricted their participation in the labor force in the MENA region. As table 7.1 shows, illiteracy rates for females in all the countries in the region are higher than males. This is particularly the case in countries such as Egypt (56%), Iraq (76%), Morocco (62%), Sudan (51%), and Yemen (71%). Countries that have made significant progress in lowering the illiteracy rates of females include Israel (7%), Qatar (15%), Bahrain (15%), and Jordan (14%).

As for female participation in the labor force, all the countries in the Middle East and North Africa (MENA) region have more males than females in the labor market. Countries that have significant numbers of females in the labor force include Israel (42%), Morocco (35%), Turkey (38%), and Kuwait (32%).

Table 7.1
Literacy Rates and Women's Participation in the Labor Force in the MENA Countries, 2002

Country	Percent Illiteracy Rates (ages 15 and over)		Female Labor Force Participation (% of total, 2002)
	Male	Female	
Algeria	22	40	29
Bahrain	8	15	—
Egypt	33	56	31
Iran	16	30	28
Iraq	44	76	20
Israel	3	7	42
Jordan	4	14	26
Kuwait	15	19	32
Lebanon	7	18	30
Libya	8	29	24
Morocco	37	62	35
Oman	18	35	19
Qatar	19	15	—
Saudi Arabia	16	31	18
Sudan	29	51	30
Syria	9	26	28
Tunisia	17	37	32
Turkey	7	25	38
United Arab Emirates	24	19	16
Yemen	31	71	28

Source: Rowntree, Lewis, Price, & Wyckoff (2006).

Of course, this is not the only region or realm in the world where the education of females and their participation in the labor force have always lagged behind males. Among the ancient Greeks, the education boys received was different from that of girls. Boys usually received education that prepared them to be soldiers or defenders of their nation. Girls, on the other hand, were prepared to play feminine roles in the society similar to those that women in the Middle East and North Africa do. In ancient Rome, boys stayed longer in school to prepare for leadership roles. Some of the upper-class boys attended specially designed schools called the *ludi*. These schools used curricula that prepared the boys for leadership roles.

In Ghana, Nigeria, and Kenya, the situation was the same. Parents always placed a higher premium on the education of boys over girls because of the potential higher returns to the investment made in the education of boys. In Southeast Asia, the desire of parents to educate only their male children was very strong, because boys were considered capable of getting the family out of poverty. It was common to hear to hear people in the community wishing newly wedded women to be mothers of ''a hundred sons.''

In North America, for more than two hundred years, girls were denied access to equal education. It was a popular belief that ''women attending high school and college were at risk because the blood destined for the development and health of their ovaries would be redirected to their brains'' (Sadker & Sadker, 2005, p. 459). Too much schooling and learning was therefore thought to be harmful to the physical and social well-being of women. One way of saving women from the damaging effects of rigorous academic programs was to enroll them in less demanding academic subjects such as singing, music, drawing, needlework, cooking, dancing, reading, and writing. Courses in science, mathematics, philosophy, engineering, and law were off-limits to women because the demands of these disciplines would make the life of a woman a permanent struggle between life and death.

GENDER SCHEMA THEORY

Differences in gender-role expectations are culturally determined. Although biology may play a part, the socialization process of children as they grow up plays a major part in how children see themselves as ''males'' or ''females.'' As children age, they begin to learn things and become aware of their gender-role expectations. Boys learn from their parents, peers, and other members of society that they should be tough, ready to lead, and resilient in their behavior, whereas girls are socialized to be dependent, respectful, obedient to rules, nurturing, and responsible in family affairs. Children begin to organize these experiences into what is called *gender schemas*. These later determine their behavior patterns as they grow up to be adults in their community (Berk, 1993).

Ormund (2000) has outlined major gender differences and their educational implications in his book, *Educational Psychology: Developing Learners* (see table 7.2).

Table 7.2
Gender Differences and Educational Implications

Feature	Differences and Similarities	Implications for Education
Cognitive Abilities	Boys and girls appear to have similar cognitive abilities. Girls are slightly better at verbal tasks; boys may have slightly better visual/spatial skills. Achievement differences in particular subjects are small and have become very similar in recent years.	Expect boys and girls to have similar cognitive abilities.
Physical Abilities	Before puberty, boys and girls have similar physical capabilities. Afterward, boys have an advantage in height and muscle strength.	Assume both genders have the potential for developing physical and motor skills, especially during the elementary years.
Motivation	Girls are generally more concerned about doing well in school. They tend to work harder on assignments, but also take fewer risks. Boys exert more effort on "stereotypically male" subjects such as math, science, and mechanics.	Encourage both boys and girls to excel in all subjects; avoid stereotyping.
Self-Esteem	Boys are more likely to have self-confidence in their abilities to control and to solve problems; girls are more likely to see themselves as more competent in interpersonal relationships. Boys have a tendency to rate their own performance more positively than girls, even when actual performance is the same.	Show all students that they can be successful in counter-stereotypical subject areas.
Career Aspirations	Girls tend to see themselves as college bound more than boys. Boys, however, have higher long-term expectations for themselves, particularly in stereotypically "masculine" areas. Girls tend to choose careers that will not interfere with a future role as wife or mother.	Expose all students to successful male and female models in all fields. Point out people who successfully juggle careers and families.
Interpersonal Relationships	Boys tend to exhibit more physical aggression; girls tend to be more affiliative and form more intimate relationships. Boys feel more comfortable in competitive situations; girls prefer cooperative environments.	Teach both genders less aggressive ways to interact and provide cooperative environments to accommodate girl's affiliative tendencies.

Source: Arends (2004, p. 80).

Despite the perceived differences between genders, available evidence indicates that both male and female students are capable of studying similar courses at schools. The differences in boys' and girls' academic preferences are simply one of the results of sex-role stereotyping that have been over the years separating men and women in the academic domain. Although progress has been made in all societies bridging the gap between male and female academic work, a lot remains to be done to level the field. As Sadker and Sadker (2004) have observed:

A "glass wall" still keeps women from the most lucrative careers and keeps men from entering traditionally female jobs. Even in careers in which tremendous progress has been made, such as medicine and law, a second generation of bias persist. In both professions, women find themselves channeled into the least prestigious, least profitable areas. (p. 460)

GOVERNMENT LEGISLATION TO PROVIDE EQUAL EDUCATIONAL OPPORTUNITIES FOR BOYS AND GIRLS

In the Middle East and North Africa, all governments have made tremendous efforts to provide schooling for all children, irrespective of gender. For example, the Jordanian constitution and 1990 National Charter guarantee the right of all Jordanian citizens to equal educational opportunity. Education Law No. 16 of 1964 and the 1994 Education Law No. 3 "stipulate social justice and equal opportunities for all Jordanians, and that education is a social necessity and the right of everyone" (Jordan, 2004, p. 39). In line with these provisions, the Jordanian government has revised the images of women in textbooks to reflect their roles as teachers, scientists, writers, and partners of men.

Article 29 of the Constitution of Kuwait states "that all citizens are equal in duties and rights, no difference between them in regard of no differences between males and females when enrolling to all stages of education and the different specializations" (Kuwait, 2004, p. 49). This constitutional provision has resulted in more women enrolling in schools and signing up for courses that are traditionally reserved for men.

Article 7 of the Bahraini constitution also guarantees the right of all citizens to equal educational opportunity (Bahrain, 2004, p. 47). The education of both male and female students receives "equal" attention from the Ministry of Education. Although there are separate public schools for boys and girls, it is common to see women managing and teaching in boys-only schools. This is an attempt on the part of the government to change the image of females as being capable of managing only house duties.

In Libya, Law No. 20 of 1991 states that all citizens in Libya, "males and females, are free and enjoy equal rights" (Libya, 2004, p. 38). To achieve gender equality in educational opportunity, the Libyan government has since 1991 introduced strategies that have enabled more girls to attend school. These include:

1. Ensuring that education stays free of charge for all stages and levels.
2. Emphasizing the obligation of education for the basic education stage.

3. The horizontal distribution of educational institutions on all parts and districts of Libya.
4. Variation of education and sub-dividing its specializations and improving the teaching methods and curriculums. (Libya, 2004, p. 38)

These measures have led to improvements in the enrollment rates of both males and females in different educational settings.

Generally in the Middle East and North Africa, most of the students who drop out of school live in the rural areas. Students in the urban areas often have a better opportunity to stay in school longer and graduate. This trend appears to be universal (see table 7.3). From table 7.3, it is clear that generally students in rural areas in several countries are at a disadvantage in terms of access to education. This is particularly the case for girls, who are usually expected to stay out of school to help provide for family needs (World Bank, 2004).

Egypt

The government of Egypt has developed an elaborate program to promote education for girls. Article 40 of the Egyptian constitution guarantees equal public rights and duties for all citizens. To this end, the government has come out with special programs to boost the schooling practices of females. These include constructing more schools in all rural areas for the purpose of making schools available to all girls, especially those outside cities.

One type of school in Egypt is what is called the "one-classroom school." These were started in the 1975/1976 school year. The schools had 25,899 students distributed across 868 schools, mostly in the remote areas of the country. These facilities educate girls and boys who might have dropped out of school for one reason or another. One-classroom schools offer children in remote areas a second chance to improve upon their literacy skills. Teachers in these schools are given special incentives such are higher salaries to teach

Table 7.3
International Comparisons: School Dropouts by Area of Residence (%)

Region	Total	Urban	Rural	Urban/Rural	Rural/Urban
CEE/CIS	11.8	10.7	12.9	−2.2	1.20
East Asia and the Pacific	12.4	8.4	14.3	−5.9	1.70
South Asia	25.7	18.2	28.1	−9.9	1.54
Middle East and North Africa	24.3	16.5	32.0	−15.5	1.94
West and Central Africa	44.2	27.9	50.8	−22.9	1.82
Eastern and Southern Africa	38.8	22.0	42.4	−20.4	1.93
Latin America and the Caribbean	8.4	6.4	12.0	−5.7	1.89
Total (countries with survey data)	*26.0*	*17.5*	*30.0*	*−12.5*	*1.71*

Source: UNICEF (2005).

in these schools. The students are given certificates when they complete their course.

Another type of schools set up to help bridge the gap between male and female student educational opportunities are the community schools. Community schools were developed by the Egyptian Ministry of Education and UNICEF. They are generally set up at rural areas to enable children in deprived areas have access to good education. The number of community schools for the 2002/2003 academic year was about 202.

Small schools are also set up specifically to help provide education for girls, and not necessarily only in rural areas. They are established in communities by the local people with the approval of the government. Their curriculum includes life-skill activities such as cooking, washing, and dress making. The girls also learn to read and write.

These government intervention activities in Egypt have led to a dramatic increase in the number of children, especially girls, enrolled in primary schools.

Turkey

Another country in the MENA region that has made tremendous strides in bridging the gap between male and female educational opportunities is Turkey. In the Republic of Turkey, the 1982 constitution ensures equal access to education for all citizens. The right of every citizen to receive education is guaranteed by Article 42. Primary education is compulsory for all citizens, females as well as males. Equality of educational opportunity for all citizens is also protected by Turkish Basic Law on National Education, No. 1739 of 1973. The basic laws promote coeducation, secularism, equal educational opportunity for all citizens, democratic education, and school–family cooperation (Turkey, 2004, p. 3).

Education Law 4702 of 2001 extended the compulsory school attendance to eight years and compels girls to stay in school at least until the age of 14 or 15. Children begin school at the age of 6, so eight years of compulsory schooling gives them the opportunity to stay in school until they are at least fourteen years of age. This provision prevents girls from dropping out of school early to marry, a practice that is common in Turkey and elsewhere in the region, especially in the rural areas.

These laws have given more girls in Turkey the opportunity to enroll in public as well as private schools to pursue their academic goals. For instance, the enrollment ratio for girls in the 1997/1998 school year was 78.9 percent, whereas the enrollment ratio for boys was 90.9 percent for the same period. For the 1990/2000 academic year, the enrollment ratio was 89.8 percent for girls and 94.4 percent for boys, and for 2003/2004, the ratios were 95.7 percent and 100.5 percent, respectively.

To increase the participation in the education system of all children, especially those in the rural areas, the Turkish government has set up of a number of rural boarding schools. These are called Regional Primary Boarding Schools

Table 7.4
Enrollments in Rural Boarding Schools in Turkey, 2004

Year	Regional Primary Boarding Schools				Boarding Primary Education Schools			
	Number	Girls	Boys	Total	Number	Girls	Boys	Total
1996/1997	143	12,483	52,782	65,265	27	208	2,244	2,452
1998/1999	184	16,183	61,189	77,372	117	2,940	7,210	10,150
1999/2000	223	18,549	69,223	87,772	167	4,551	12,437	16,988
2000/2001	270	27,826	87,560	115,386	237	10,009	21,621	31,630
2001/2002	282	31,728	87,395	119,123	241	12,659	25,822	38,481
2002/2003	287	34,040	89,339	123,379	260	14,151	29,033	43,184
2003/2004	290	36,666	86,625	123,291	274	16,545	30,622	47,167

Source: Turkey (2004, p. 22).

(YIBO) and Boarding Primary Education Schools (PIO). These schools provide educational opportunities for thousands of children in the country (see table 7.4).

GENDER AND SCHOOLING IN ISRAEL

Like the rest of the MENA countries, Israel has made significant progress in promoting gender equality in schooling. Both boys and girls attend the same school and sit in the same classroom with other students. In other words, the state promotes coeducation. Although there are separate schools for boys and girls, the general impression is that the state has no strict rules concerning the organization of schools in terms of gender. The orthodox community, however, prefers separate schools for boys and girls, especially above the elementary level. The main reason for this is based in religion.

During the academic year 2005, the enrollment of both boys and girls in preprimary, primary, and secondary institutions appeared to be equal. At the tertiary level, however, the number of women enrolled was more than the number of men who had enrolled to pursue different academic programs.

Boys and girls are not required to wear uniforms in state schools. They are free to wear any appropriate and comfortable clothes to school just as students do in public schools in the United States. In the private sectors, schools may require students to wear uniforms.

GENDER DIFFERENCES AND SCHOOLING IN THE MIDDLE EAST AND NORTH AFRICA: PRE-UNIVERSITY EDUCATION

Gender differences have resulted in variances in the schooling practices of male and female students in the Middle East and North Africa since the dawn of history. For many years, tradition forbade teaching girls reading and writing skills. Even when girls had access to schooling, society expected them to follow different curricula. As Heyworth-Dunne (1938) has pointed out, "The art of music and dancing were not taught to women as they were considered incompatible with decency" (p. 15). These areas were best left for only professionals. Physical education was another course girls were not expected to be taught at school. The idea here was not to subject girls to laborious activities while at school.

Although the practice has seen significant changes in recent years, there are traces of gendered programs all over the MENA region. In Bahrain, for instance, for the 2004/2005 academic year, girls in secondary schools within an applied curriculum track were not allowed to take courses in agriculture and livestock or hotel management; boys could not take courses in textile and clothing or graphic design. These arrangements were made to provide students with the skills they needed to play appropriate social roles as adults.

General education is provided in three main categories:

- Boys-only schools
- Girls-only schools
- Coeducational schools (boys and girls mixed)

Boys-Only Schools

In the MENA region, it has long been a tradition to keep males and females apart for social activities such as schooling (Heyworth-Dunne, 1938). Although the situation may differ from country to country, the general practice is that the gender line still prevails when it comes to organizing activities. All the countries in the region have boys-only schools in all the major cities, towns, and villages. Boys-only schools are usually government-controlled educational institutions. These are numerous everywhere, especially in Saudi Arabia, where the practice of separating boys and girls for differential education is rigidly observed. Boys schools may be day or boarding schools.

The Rashid School for Boys in Dubai, United Arab Emirates, is a famous international institution in the region. Opened in 1986, the Rashid School is a private school controlled by British administrators and local officials. The curriculum follows the British model, with the exception that students learn other languages such as Arabic and Arab history and culture. The school prepares students to study in American, British, and other European institutions of higher learning. Courses taught in the school are subject to approval from the government.

Girls-Only Schools

Girls-only schools exist to provide appropriate education for girls. Again, these may be day or boarding schools. The curriculum may be the same as that found in schools for boys, but the emphasis on certain subjects such as agricultural science and engineering may differ from country to country and from school to school. Many of the girls-only schools are supported by governments. Few are supported by private organizations.

One example is the Latifa School for Girls in Dubai. It is a day school that was founded by the government of Dubai in 1982. The Latifa School admits girls between ages 3 and 18. This means that girls can attend preschool there and continue to study in the school until they are ready for college. As at the Rashid School for Boys, the curriculum follows essentially British standards since the school prepares students to enter higher education institutions in foreign countries such as the United States or United Kingdom. The school curriculum is also approved by the government of the United Arab Emirates. Students who wish to study abroad often take the following courses during their sixth form (senior year):

- English Literature
- Mathematics
- Biology
- Chemistry
- Physics
- French
- Arabic
- Geography
- Art and Design

Students who wish to study in American or European universities need to get good advanced-level passes in the above subjects during the General School Certificate Examinations (GSCE).

In an effort to immerse students in the Arab culture, girls at the Latifa School study Arab history, the Arabic language, and Islamic studies. The students are also taught leadership skills and how to cooperate with others to achieve group goals. The Latifa School has modern facilities, including a well-developed library, swimming pool, computers, exercise facilities, and playgrounds. Girls play games such as netball and volleyball and also engage in track and field events.

Coeducation

Many of the countries in the MENA region do not support coeducation after the third grade. In kindergarten, it is common to see boys and girls studying together. In the classroom, boys sit on one side of the room and girls occupy the other side. However, after the third grade, the two sexes go to different schools. Coeducation is essentially provided only by foreign institutions. Great Britain, the United States, Germany, France, and Australia all have private educational institutions providing coeducational facilities for thousands of students.

The Dubai British School is one such school that provides coeducation for students in the region. It was established in 2005 to provide Western and local-style education for children. Class sizes are generally small. Foundation classes may have a maximum of sixteen students; primary and secondary classes may have up to twenty-two.

The school is organized into "foundations" and "key stages." The foundations are meant to educate children between ages 3 and 5. The curriculum focuses on basic concepts in learning, providing children with basic education skills in the areas of reading, writing, computing, and educational technology. Key stages provide education for students through age 18. Students at this level learn details of each subject in the school curriculum. It is from this level that students are prepared for matriculation and for college and university education.

The Dubai British School curriculum is based upon British, Scottish, and local standards. Courses available at the school include:

- Arabic
- Art
- Biology
- Business Studies
- Chemistry
- Design Technology
- Drama
- Economics
- English
- French
- Geography
- German
- History
- Information Communication and Technology
- Mathematics
- Media Studies
- Music
- Physical Education
- Physics
- Sociology
- Spanish

Modernization of the education system has indeed made several courses and school activities available to girls in all schools in the United Arab Emirates. Girls can study music, drama, and physical education. They do, in fact, read and write. All students, irrespective of gender, have the right to enroll in a subject of their choice. Boys, for instance, can enroll in a home economics class if they wish. Girls, on the other hand, may enroll in courses in agriculture or woodwork, courses traditionally reserved for boys in many of the public schools in the region.

School Uniforms

All students attending the Dubai British School are required to wear pre-scribed uniforms to school. Students who do not dress appropriately for classes may be asked by the school principal to go home for the proper uniform. Boys and girls participate in physical education activities. They must wear approved clothing during physical education lessons.

Boys and girls wear different uniforms. Juniors, and Foundations to Key Stage Six, wear white, short-sleeve, polo-style shirts with logo. Boys wear navy Bermuda shorts, and girls at this stage wear tartan skirts. Boys in the secondary division wear a white shirt with button-down collar and logo, navy trousers, and a tartan tie. Girls wear a white shirt and navy skirt.

The Internet

Students in the Dubai British School have access to the Internet. The computers in the Dubai British School library and the Information Communication Technology center have been connected to the Internet, and students use them for their schoolwork. Students must sign acceptable-use policy forms before being allowed to use the Internet (Dubai British School, 2007).

WHAT GIRLS AND BOYS ARE STUDYING IN MIDDLE EASTERN AND NORTH AFRICAN SCHOOLS

Generally, boys and girls study similar subjects at the elementary level. However, as they move up the educational ladder, the curricula for boys and girls change in a few areas. In some cases, especially in Saudi Arabia, girls are not encouraged to engage in physical education in public schools. In Syria, when girls study home economics or needlework, boys study agriculture (see tables 7.5 and 7.6).

Of course, this arrangement is also common in many other countries. In Ghana and Nigeria, for example, boys generally do not study home economics or needlework. While the girls study these subjects in specially designed buildings, the boys engage in other activities such as carpentry, woodwork, cloth making, or agriculture.

At the higher education levels, men and women study similar subjects, but there are some areas that men do not often see as befitting their gender role. One such area is nursing. In most cases, the majority of students enrolled in nursing are women.

Women in the region are usually outnumbered by men in the engineering, manufacturing, and construction disciplines. In Jordan, for the 2004 academic year, in the areas of engineering, manufacturing, and construction, only about 10 percent of the students were women. A similar picture emerges in Morocco.

The participation of women in the social sciences, education, service, and health areas depicts a different picture. This is because these areas are traditionally seen by many as female domains (UNICEF, 2005).

Table 7.5
Weekly Lesson Timetable, Preparatory Education (Lower Secondary), Syria, 2002

Subject	Number of weekly periods in each form		
	I	II	III
Religious education	2	2	2
Arabic language (including handwriting)	6	6	6
Foreign language	5	5	5
Mathematics	4	4	5
Social studies (history, geography, and national socialist education)	4	4	4
General science	3	4	4
Drawing	1	1	1
Practical subjects (manual works)	2	2	1
Music and anthems	1	2	–
Agriculture (boys) or needlework and home economics (girls)	2	2	2
Military training	2	2	2
Total weekly periods	*32*	*34*	*32*
Physical education (boys)	2	2	2
Physical education (girls)	2	2	1

Source: International Bureau of Education, http://www.ibe.unesco.org/.countries/country Dossier/timestables/TSyrianAR.pdf.

Table 7.6
Weekly Lesson Timetable, Preparatory Education (Lower Secondary), Qatar, 2002

Subject	Number of weekly periods in each form					
	I		II		III	
	Boys	Girls	Boys	Girls	Boys	Girls
Religious studies	5	5	5	5	5	5
Arabic language	7	7	7	7	7	7
English language	6	6	6	6	6	6
Mathematics	5	5	5	5	5	5
Hygiene and general science	4	3	4	3	4	3
Social studies	4	4	4	4	4	4
Fine arts	3	2	3	2	3	2
Home economics	—	2	—	2	—	2
Physical education	2	2	2	2	2	2

Source: International Bureau of Education, http://www.ibe.unesco.org/.countries/country Dossier/timestables/TSyrianAR.pdf.

CONCLUSION

Many of the countries in the MENA region have over the last decade devoted substantial resources to promoting education, especially for females (UNICEF, 2004). According to the World Bank (2004), countries in the Middle East and North Africa altogether during the last decade spent more than 5.3 percent of gross domestic product on education—the highest in the world (World Bank, 2004).

As is clear from table 7.7, countries in the Middle East and North Africa have made extensive progress in making education available to all children in the region. Girls in particular have benefited a great deal from this regional effort. The number of children out of primary school by gender in the region is now comparable to other regions such as South Asia, and far better than what transpires in Sub-Saharan Africa.

At the secondary level, the enrollment gap between boys and girls is smaller. The enrollment rate for girls is 74 percent for girls and for boys is 77 percent. This is an impressive record, bearing in mind that about twenty years ago, the education of girls in the region received little or no attention from most of the governments in the region (World Bank, 2004).

In the area of tertiary education, more women are enrolling in various courses to obtain higher education credentials. As the World Bank (2004) has observed:

Across the region more than one in four girls now enrolls in tertiary education, and women outnumber men in colleges and universities in several countries of the region. Girls who stay in school tend to outperform boys. But data on school completion show much higher dropout rates for girls at all levels, predominantly because of early marriages. (p. 7)

Table 7.7
International Comparisons: School Dropouts by Gender and Region (%)

| | Children out of primary school (%) by gender and region | | | | |
Region	Total	Male	Female	Male/ Female	Female/ Male
CEE/CIS	11.8	11.3	12.3	−1.0	1.09
East Asia and the Pacific	12.4	12.7	12.1	0.6	0.95
South Asia	25.7	22.4	29.0	−6.6	1.29
Middle East and North Africa	24.3	20.8	27.9	−7.1	1.34
West and Central Africa	44.2	40.6	47.9	−7.3	1.18
Eastern and Southern Africa	38.8	38.6	39.0	−0.3	1.01
Latin America and the Caribbean	8.4	8.6	8.2	0.4	0.96
Total (based on 80 developing countries with survey data)	*26.0*	*24.1*	*28.1*	*−4.0*	*1.17*

Source: World Bank (2004).

It is the view of many educators that the influx of foreign schools in the region will help narrow, if not eliminate completely, the gap that exists between the educational opportunities for male and female students in most of the countries in the Middle East and North Africa.

REFERENCES

Arends, R. I. (2004). *Learning to teach* (6th ed.). Boston: McGraw-Hill.

Bahrain, Ministry of Education. (2004). *Development of education in Bahrain*. Report presented to the 47th session of the International Conference on Education, Geneva, September 8–11. Available at http://www.ibe.unesco.org/International/ICE47/English/Natreps/reports/bahrain_en_part_1.pdf.

Berk, L. E. (1993). *Infants, children, and adolescents*. Boston: Allyn & Bacon.

Dubai British School (2007). *Parent handbook, 2006–2007*. Dubai: Author.

Heyworth-Dunne, J. (1938). *An introduction to the history of education in modern Egypt*. London: Luzac.

Jordan. Ministry of Education. (2004). *The development of education: National report of the Hashemite Kingdom of Jordan*. Report presented to the 47th session of the International Conference on Education, Geneva, September 8–11. Available at http://www.ibe.unesco.org/International/ICE47/English/Natreps/reports/jordan.pdf.

Kuwait. Ministry of Education. (2004). *The national report about the development of education process in the state of Kuwait*. Report presented to the 47th session of the International Conference on Education, Geneva, September 8–11. Available at http://www.ibe.unesco.org/International/ICE47/English/Natreps/reports/kuwait_part_2_en.pdf.

Libya. Libyan National Commission for Education, Culture, and Science. (2004). *The development of education in the Great Jamahiriya*. Report presented to the 47th session of the International Conference on Education, Geneva, September 8–11. Available at http://www.ibe.unesco.org/International/ICE47/English/Natreps/reports/libya_en.pdf.

Ormund, J. E. (2000). *Educational psychology: Developing learners* (3rd ed.). Upper Saddle River, NJ: Merrill.

Rowntree, L., Lewis, M., Price, M., & Wyckoff, W. (2006). *Diversity amid globalization: World regions, environment, development* (3rd ed.). Upper Saddle River, NJ: Pearson Prentice Hall.

Sadker, M. P., & Sadker, D. M. (2005). *Teachers, schools, and society*. Boston: McGraw-Hill.

Turkey. Ministry of National Education. (2004). *The Turkish education system and development in education, 2004*. Report presented to the 47th session of the International Conference on Education, Geneva, September 8–11. Available at http://www.ibe.unesco.org/International/ICE47/English/Natreps/reports/turkey.pdf.

UNICEF. (2004). *Progress for children: A report card on gender parity and education (2)*. New York: Author.

———. (2005). *Levels, trends, and determinants of primary school participation and gender parity*. New York: Author.

World Bank. (2004). *Gender and development in the Middle East and North Africa: Women in the public sphere*. Washington, DC: Author.

BIBLIOGRAPHY

Ainscow, M. (1997). Towards inclusive schooling. *British Journal of Special Education, 24*(1), 3–6.

AIU Library Newsletter. (May, 2005). Database usage statistics. *Mahammad IV Library Newsletter, 2*, 2.

Akkari, A. (2004). Education in the Middle East and North Africa: The current situation and future challenges. *International Education Journal, 5*(2), 144–53.

Al-Abed, A. B. (1986). Educational technology in the Arab World. *International Review of Education, 32*(3), 350–53.

Al Akhawayn University. (2005a). *Al Akhawayn University in Ifrane, 2005–2007 Catalog.* Rabat: Imprimerie el Maarif al Jadida. Available at http://www.aui.ma/DSA/academic-catalog-07-general.pdf.

———. (2005b). Database usage statistics. *Muhammad IV Library Newsletter, 2* (May), 2.

Alghazo, E. M., & Naggar, E. E. (2004). General education teachers in the United Arab Emirates and their acceptance of the inclusion of students with disabilities. *British Journal of Special Education, 31*(2), 94–99.

Al-Shammari, Z., & Yawkey, T. D. (2007). Examining the development and recommendations for special education in the state of Kuwait: An evolving program. *Education, 127*(4), 534–40.

American International School. (2007). *High school profile 2007–2008.* Even Yehuda, Israel.

Anderson, L. (1984). Nineteenth-century reform in Ottoman Libya. *International Journal of Middle Eastern Studies, 16*(3), 325–48.

Angelides, P. A., Stylianou, T., & Gibbs, P. (2006). Preparing teachers for inclusive education in Cyprus. *Teaching and Teacher Education, 22*, 513–22.

Arends, R. I. (2004). *Learning to teach* (6th ed.). Boston: McGraw-Hill.

Bahgat, G. (1999). Education in the Gulf monarchies: Retrospect and prospect. *International Review of Education, 45*(2), 127–36.

Bahrain. (1996). *Bahrain*. Report presented to the 45th session of the International Conference on Education, Geneva, September 30–October 5. Available at http://www.ibe.unesco.org/countries/countryDossier/natrep96/bahrain96.pdf.

Bahrain, Ministry of Education. (2004). *Development of education in Bahrain*. Report presented to the 47th session of the International Conference on Education, Geneva, September 8–11. Available at http://www.ibe.unesco.org/International/ICE47/English/Natreps/reports/bahrain_en_part_1.pdf.

Balch, T. W. (1909). French colonization in North Africa. *American Political Science Review, 3*(4), 539–51.

Beller, M. (2001). Admission to higher education in Israel and the role of psychometric entrance test: Educational and political dilemma. *Assessment in Education, 8*(3), 315–37.

Berk, L. E. (1993). *Infants, children, and adolescents*. Boston: Allyn & Bacon.

Boyle, H. N. (2006). Memorization and learning in Islamic schools. *Comparative Education Review, 50*(3), 478–95.

Brewer, D. J., & Teeter, E. (1999). *Egypt and the Egyptians*. Cambridge: Cambridge University Press.

British International School. (2006). British International School Internet policy. Riyadh, Saudi Arabia: Author.

Burrows, M. (1986). "Mission civilisatrice": French cultural policy in the Middle East, 1860–1914. *Historical Journal, 29*(1), 109–35.

Caldwell, W. E., & Gyles, M. F. (1966). *The ancient world*. New York: Holt, Rinehart, & Winston.

Calvert, J. R., & Al-Shetaiwi, A. S. (2002). Exploring the mismatch between skills and jobs for women in Saudi Arabia in technical and vocational areas: The view of Saudi Arabian private sector business managers. *International Journal of Training and Development, 6*(2), 112–24.

Cavkaytar, A. (2006). Teacher training on special education in Turkey. *Turkish Online Journal of Educational Technology, 5*(3), Article 7, http://www.tojet.net/volumes/v5i3.pdf.

Clark, N. (2006). Education in Morocco. *World Education News & Reviews, 10*(2), 1.

Cook, B. J. (2000). Egypt's national education debate. *Comparative Education, 36*(4), 477–90.

Courtney-Clark, M. (1996). *Imazighen: The vanishing traditions of the Berber women*. New York: Clarkson Potter.

Danino, M. (2006). In the absence of a law to protect their rights, Israeli students with learning disabilities fall between the cracks. Paper presented at the Learning Disabilities Association of America national conference, Jacksonville, Florida, March. Available at http://eng.nitzan-israel.org.il/learning_disabilities_in_israel_nitzan_ld.

de Blij, H. J., & Muller, P. O. (2007). *The world today: Concepts and regions in geography*. Atlantic Highlands, NJ: John Wiley.

Diab, H., & Wåhlin, L. (1950). The geography of education in Syria in 1882. With a translation of "Education in Syria" by Shahin Makarius, 1883. *Geografisker Annaler*, series B. *Human Geography, 65*(2), 105–28.

Dreikurs, R., & Soltz, V. (1990). *Children: The challenge*. New York: Plume.

Dubai British School (2007). *Parent handbook, 2006–2007*. Dubai: Author.

Easton, S. C. (1964). *The heritage of the past: From the earliest times to 1500*. New York: Holt, Rinehart, & Winston.

Egypt. (2004). *Development of Education in Arab Republic of Egypt, 2000–2004.* Cairo: Author.

Egypt. National Center for Educational Research and Development. (2001). *Education development: National report of Arab Republic of Egypt from 1990–2000.* Cairo: Author.

Elazar, D. J. (1990). *Israel's education system: An introduction to a study program.* Jerusalem: Institute for the Study of Educational Systems.

Elmenoufy, S. G. (2007). Mathematics education for the gifted in Egypt. *Proceedings of the British Society for Research into Learning Mathematics, 27*(2). Available at http://www.bsrlm.org.uk/IPs/ip27-2/BSRLM-IP-27-2-03.pdf.

El-Tawil, E. A. (1984). The relative effects of certified teachers on their pupils' achievement. *School Psychology International, 5,* 103–6.

Faksh, M. A. (1976). An historical survey of the educational system in Egypt. *International Review of Education, 22*(2), 234–44.

Friend, M. (2005). *Special education: Contemporary perspectives for school professionals.* Boston: Pearson.

Gaad, E. (2004). Cross-cultural perspectives on the effect of cultural attitudes towards inclusion for children with intellectual disabilities. *Journal of Inclusive Education, 8*(3), 311–28.

Gagné, R. M., Wager, W. W., Golas, K. C., & Keller, J. M. (2005). *Principles of instructional design.* Belmont, CA: Wadsworth.

Gerner, M. (1985). The school psychologist in Saudi Arabia. *School Psychology International, 6,* 88–94.

Goldgraber, Y. (1997). Special education in Israel. http://www.kinneret.co.il/ben zev/yacov/spedartc.htm.

Hartt, F. (1993). *Art: A history of painting, sculpture, architecture.* Englewood Cliffs, NJ: Prentice-Hall.

Hawkins, J. D. (1979). The origin and dissemination of writing in Western Asia. In M. P. R. S. Moorey (Ed.), *The origins of civilization: Wolfson College lectures, 1978.* Oxford, England: Clarendon.

Heggoy, A. A. (1973). Education in French Algeria: An essay on cultural conflict. *Comparative Education Review, 17*(2), 180–97.

Heggoy, A. A., & Zingg, P. J. (1976). French education in revolutionary North Africa. *International Journal of Middle East Studies, 7*(4), 571–78.

Herrera, L. (2003). Participation in school upgrading: Gender, class and (in)action in Egypt. *International Journal of Educational Development, 23,* 187–99.

Heyworth-Dunne, J. (1938). *An introduction to the history of education in modern Egypt.* London: Luzac.

Hourani, A. (2002). *A history of the Arab peoples.* Cambridge, MA: Harvard University Press.

International Bureau of Education (2008). http://www.ibe.unesco.org/coun tries/WDE/2006/WESTERN-EUROPE/Israel/Israel.pdf.

Israel. (1996). *Israel: National report, 1996.* Report presented to the 45th session of the International Conference on Education, Geneva, September 30–October 5. Available at http://www.ibe.unesco.org/countries/countryDossier/natrep96/israel96.pdf.

Israel. Ministry of Education, Culture, and Sport. (2004). *Facts and figures*. Jerusalem: Author.

Israel Science and Technology (2008). Available at http://www.science.co.il/Univ.asp.

JDC-Brookdale Institute. (2004). *People with disability in Israel: Facts and figures*. Disability Research Unit, Avital Sandler-Loeff (JDC—Israel), Unit for Disabilities and Rehabilitation.

Jewish Agency for Israel. (2008). The ABC's of education in Israel, part 1. Available from http://www.jewishagency.org/JewishAgency/English/Aliyah/Aliyah+Info/ Thoughts+on+Aliyah+and+Israel/Articles+about+Israel/Education+in+Israel+-+part+1.htm.

Johnson, J. A., Dupuis, V. L., Musial, D., Hall, G. E., & Gollnick, D. M. (2005). *Introduction to the foundations of American education*. Boston: Allyn & Bacon.

Jordan. Ministry of Education. (2004). *The development of education: National report of the Hashemite Kingdom of Jordan*. Report presented to the 47th session of the International Conference on Education, Geneva, September 8–11. Available at http://www.ibe.unesco.org/International/ICE47/English/Natreps/reports/jordan.pdf.

Kinsey, D. C. (1971). Efforts for educational synthesis under colonial rule: Egypt and Tunisia. *Comparative Education Review, 15*(2), 172–87.

Kurian, G. T. (1988). *Israel*, in *World Education Encyclopedia*, vol. 2. New York: Facts on File, 636–47.

Kuwait. Ministry of Education. (2004). *The national report about the development of education process in the state of Kuwait*. Report presented to the 47th session of the International Conference on Education, Geneva, September 8–11. Available at http://www.ibe.unesco.org/International/ICE47/English/Natreps/reports/kuwait_part_2_en.pdf.

Langhor, V. (2005). Colonial educational systems and the spread of local religious movements: The cases of British Egypt and Punjab. *Society for Comparative Study of Society and History, 47*, 161–89.

Libyan National Commission for Development of Education, Culture, and Science. (2004). *The development of education in the great Jamahiriya*. A National report presented to the International Conference on Education, Session 47, 8–11 September, Geneva. Available at http://www.ibe.unesco.org/International/ICE47/English/Natreps/reports/libya_en.pdf.

Lulat, Y. G-M. (2005). *A history of African higher education from antiquity to the present*. Westport, CT: Praeger.

Mba, P. O. (1983). Trends in education of the handicapped children in developing countries with particular reference to Africa. *B.C. Journal of Special Education, 7*(3), 273–78.

Meadan, H., & Gumpel, T. P. (2002). Special education in Israel. *Council for Exceptional Children, 34*(5), 16–20.

Metz, H. D. (Ed.). (1992). *Saudi Arabia: A country study*. Washington, DC: GPO.

Ministry of Immigrant Absorption, (2005). *Education*. Author.

Mizikaci, F. (2006). *Higher education in Turkey*. UNESCO-CEPES Monographs on Higher Education. Bucharest, Romania: UNESCO European Center for Higher Education.

Monk, M., Swain, J., Ghrist, M., & Riddle, W. (2003). Notes on classroom practice and ownership and use of personal computers amongst Egyptian science and mathematics teachers. *Education and Information Technologies, 8*(1), 83–95.

Mott, P. E. (1965). *The organization of society.* Englewood Cliffs, NJ: Prentice-Hall.

Nasser, R. (2004). Exclusion and the making of Jordanian national identity: An analysis of school textbooks. *Nationalism and Ethnic Politics, 10,* 221–49.

Oliva, P. F. (2005). *Developing the curriculum.* Boston: Pearson.

Ormund, J. E. (2000). *Educational psychology: Developing learners* (3rd ed.). Upper Saddle River, NJ: Merrill.

Parsons, R. D., Hinson, S. L., & Sardo-Brown, D. (2001). *Educational psychology: A practitioner-researcher model of teaching.* Belmont, CA: Wadsworth.

Peyser, M. (2005). Identifying and nurturing gifted children in Israel. *International Journal for the Advancement of Counseling, 27*(2), 229–43.

Potter, W. N. (1961). Modern education in Syria. *Comparative Education Review, 5*(1), 35–38.

Qatar. Supreme Education Council. Evaluation Institute. (2006). *Schools and schooling in Qatar, 2004–2006.* Available at http://www.english.education.gov.qa.

Qubain, F. I. (1966). *Education and science in the Arab world.* Baltimore: Johns Hopkins University Press.

Rathus, S. A. (1993). *Psychology* (5th ed.). Fort Worth, TX: Harcourt Brace Jovanovich College Publishers.

Reid, D. M. (1983). Turn-of-the-century Egyptian school days. *Comparative Education Review, 27*(3), 374–93.

Reynolds, C. R., & Fletcher-Janzen, E. (2002). *Concise encyclopedia of special education.* New York: John Wiley & Sons.

Rowntree, L., Lewis, M., Price, M., & Wyckoff, W. (2006). *Diversity amid globalization: World regions, environment, development* (3rd ed.). Upper Saddle River, NJ: Pearson Prentice Hall.

Russell, M. (2002). Competing, overlapping, and contradictory agendas: Egyptian education under British occupation, 1882–1922. *Comparative Studies of South Asia, Africa and the Middle East, 21*(1–2), 50–60.

Sadker, M. P., & Sadker, D. M. (2005). *Teachers, schools, and society.* Boston: McGraw-Hill.

Saleh, M. A. (1986). Development of higher education in Saudi Arabia. *Higher Education, 15*(1/2), 17–23.

Salmi, U. M. (1999). Recent developments in Egyptian education. *World Education News & Reviews, 12*(5), 8–12.

Saudi Arabia. Ministry of Education. (2003). *The development of education.* Riyadh: Author.

Scott, T. M., & Shearer-Lingo, A. (2002). The effects of reading fluency instruction on the academic and behavioral success of middle school students in a self-contained EBD classroom. *Preventing School Failure, 46*(4), 167–73.

Sedgwick, R. (2001). Education in Saudi Arabia. *World Education News & Reviews, 14*(6), http://www.wes.org/ewenr/01nov/practical.htm.

Smith, D. D. (2001). *Introduction to special education: Teaching in an age of opportunity.* 4th ed. Boston: Allyn & Bacon.

Smith, T. E. C., Polloway, E. A., Patton, J. R., & Dowdy, C. A. (2006). *Teaching students with special needs in inclusive settings.* Boston: Allyn & Bacon.

Social Science Staff of the Educational Research Council of America. (1982). *The growth of civilization*. Boston: Allyn & Bacon.

Sprinzak, D., Sergev, Y., Bar, E., and Leve-Mazloum, D. (1996). *Facts and figures about education in Israel*. Jerusalem. State of Israel, Ministry of Education.

Starrett, G. (1995). The hexis of interpretation: Islam and the body in the Egyptian popular school. *American Ethnologist, 22*(4), 953–69.

Szyliowicz, J. S. (1971). Elite recruitment in Turkey: The role of the Mulkiye. *World Politics, 23*(3), 371–98.

———. (1973). *Education and modernization in the Middle East*. Ithaca, NY: Cornell University Press.

Tel Aviv University, Overseas Students Program (2008). Academic information: http://www.tau.ac.il/overseas/frameset.html.

Thompson, A. R. (1981). *Education and development in Africa*. New York: St. Martin's.

Totah, K. A. (1926). *The contribution of the Arabs to education*. New York: Teachers College Press.

Trial, G. T., & Bayly, W. (1950). Modern education in Saudi Arabia. *History of Education Journal, 1*(3), 121–33.

Turkey. Ministry of National Education. (2004). *The Turkish education system and development in education, 2004*. Report presented to the 47th session of the International Conference on Education, Geneva, September 8–11. Available at http://www.ibe.unesco.org/International/ICE47/English/Natreps/reports/turkey.pdf.

UNESCO. (1994). *The Salamanca Statement and framework for action on special needs Education*. Paris: Author.

———. (1995). *Review of the present situation in special needs education*. Paris: Author.

———. (1999). *Students with disabilities in regular schools*. Paris: Author.

———. (2005). *Guidelines for inclusion: Ensuring access to education for all*. Paris: Author.

———. (2008). *Israel: Principles and general objectives of education*. http://www.ibe.unesco.org/countries/WDE/2006/Western_Europe/Israel/Israel.pdf.

UNICEF. (2004). *Progress for children: A report card on gender parity and education (2)*. New York: Author.

———. (2005). *Levels, trends, and determinants of primary school participation and gender parity*. New York: Author.

UNESCO. Institute for Statistics. (2007). *Education Systems*. Retrieved July 1, 2007. http://stats.uis.unesco.org/unesco/TableViewer/tableView.aspx?ReportId=163.

UNESCO. International Bureau of Education. (2006). *Bahrain*. http://www.ibe.unesco.org/countries/WDE/2006/ARAB_STATES/Bahrain/Bahrain.pdf.

———. (2006). *United Arab Emirates*. http://www.ibe.unesco.org/countries/WDE/2006/ARAB_STATES/United_Arab_Emirates/United_Arab_Emirates.pdf.

———. (2006). *World Data on Education*, 6th Ed. http://www.ibe.unesco.org/countries/WDE/2006/ARAB_STATES/Jordan/Jordan.pdf.

Verma, D. (1981). Kuwait's system of technical-vocational education: An investment in future. *Community College Review, 9*(2), 53–57.

Walker, J. (2003). *One hundred things you should know about ancient Egypt*. Essex, England: Barnes & Noble.

Webb, L. D., Metha, A., & Jordan, K. F. (2000). *Foundations of American education.* Columbus, OH: Prentice-Hall.

Williams, A. (1968). *Britain and France in the Middle East and North Africa, 1914–1967.* New York: St. Martin's.

World Bank. (2004). *Gender and development in the Middle East and North Africa: Women in the public sphere.* Washington, DC: Author.

———. (2005). *Reforming technical vocational education and training in the Middle East and North Africa: Experiences and challenges.* Luxembourg: European Training Foundations.

Zigler, E. F., & Stevenson, M. F. (1993). *Children in a changing world: Development and social issues.* Pacific Grove, CA: Brooks/Cole.

INDEX

admission, 64, 67, 68, 71, 77–78, 100;
    requirements of, 58, 61, 70, 75
Ahlia University, 59
Aim Shams University, 62
Akkari, A., 52
Al Akhawayn University, 67
Al-Azhar University, 56
Alexandria, 6, 9–10
Algeria, 13–14, 44–45
alphabet, 4
ancient schools. *See* schools, ancient
The Ancient World (Caldwell and
    Gyles), 4
aphasia, 82
Arab and Druze Schools, 23
Arabic, 8, 17, 19, 41, 44
autism, 82

Baghdad, 10
Bahrain, 30, 100–101; gender, 113;
    higher education, 58–60, 72; laws of,
    57–58, 109; pre-primary schools, 47;
    school specialization, 34, 35, 36;
    secondary schools, 50; special needs
    education, 99–100, 101
behavioral problems, 82
Berbers, 13
blind students, 100–101
boys only schools, 113

Britain, 56; imperial education, 18–21, 24
British International School, 39
Burrows, M., 11
Byzantine Empire, education in, 1–2

Cairo, 10, 56, 57
Charlemagne, Emperor, 1
childhood aphasia, 82
Child and Motherhood Care Society,
    101
children. *See* learning disabilities;
    pre-primary schools; students
classroom management, 53
classrooms, 98
class size, 45
coeducational institutions, 53–54, 67,
    114–15
colleges. *See* universities
colonial education, 13–14, 24, 43,
    56–57; Britain and, 18–21, 24;
    France and, 13–14, 24; United
    States and, 24
commercial tract in school, 31, 36, 62
community school, 111
compulsory education, 48–49, 50,
    51, 111
constitutions, 109, 110
Council for Higher Education
    (Israel), 75

About the Author

KWABENA DEI OFORI-ATTAH, originally from Ghana, West Africa, is Associate Professor of Education, Capital University, Columbus, OH. He has developed a web site and online journal, *The African Symposium*, for the African Educational Research Network. It is available online at http://www.africanresearch.org.